The

RETURN

of

INTUITION

ABOUT THE AUTHOR

Kathryn Harwig has a bachelor's degree in psychology and a doctorate in law. She is a former probation officer and lawyer who now trains people in enhancing their intuitive ability. She is the author of five books, which have been published in four languages. She writes a regular monthly column for the *Edge* magazine, has been featured in television specials on A&E, TruTV, and the Discovery Channel, and is a regular guest on radio and television. Kathryn has trained thousands of people to use their intuition, and she appears at expos, conferences, and events worldwide.

KATHRYN HARWIG

....

The

RETURN

of

INTUITION

....

Llewellyn Publications
Woodbury, Minnesota

First Edition
First Printing, 2010

Cover photograph© iStockphoto.com/Tjanze (Maribor-Slovenia)
Cover design by Kevin R. Brown
Editing by Connie Hill

Llewellyn is a registered trademark of Llewellyn Worldwide Ltd.

Library of Congress Cataloging-in-Publication Data (Pending)

Harwig, Kathryn, 1951–
   The return of intuition : awakening psychic gifts in the secondhalf
of life / Kathryn Harwig. — 1st ed.
      p.   cm.
   Includes bibliographical references and index.
   ISBN: 978-0-7387-1880-4
   1. Older people—Psychic ability.   I. Title.

   BF1045.043H37   2010
   133.8084'6—dc22   2010010393

Llewellyn Worldwide Ltd. does not participate in, endorse, or have any authority or responsibility concerning private business transactions between our authors and the public.
   All mail addressed to the author is forwarded, but the publisher cannot, unless specifically instructed by the author, give out an address or phone number.
   Any Internet references contained in this work are current at publication time, but the publisher cannot guarantee that a specific location will continue to be maintained. Please refer to the publisher's website for links to authors' websites and other sources.

Llewellyn Publications
A Division of Llewellyn Worldwide Ltd.
2143 Wooddale Drive
Woodbury, MN 55125-2989
www.llewellyn.com

Printed in the United States of America

DEDICATION

This book is dedicated to the elders,
sages, crones, and wise ones.
Our intuitive wisdom can change the world.

ACKNOWLEDGMENTS

Many thanks to all of my generous and wonderful students, clients, readers, and friends who have shared their stories, their lives, and their wisdom with me.

CONTENTS

"Aging seems to be the only available way
to live a long time."

—DANIEL FRANCOIS-ESPRIT AUBER

Introduction

Grace sat in my office, tears welling in her dark brown eyes. She had lost her husband and soul mate to cancer six months before, but the tears were not because of that.

"I just can't tell anyone about this," she whispered.

David, who had been her companion and the love of her life, had died slowly, she told me. They had shared laughter and tears and life for four decades, and she missed him desperately. "But," she insisted, "I am not crazy. I may be old. I may be grieving. But I am not crazy."

Since David's death, Grace told me, she had been experiencing visible and auditory messages from him. He would also leave her little signs: pennies on the carpet, a butterfly landing on her hand, the television turning on and off.

At first, she went on, she told herself she was making it up. "Anything to comfort myself," she laughed. But, as the weeks wore into months, she began to feel his presence more and more. "He will sit on the bed at night," she continued. "I can see the indentation.

"He talks to me in my mind as well. I know his speech, his mannerisms. I know it is David and not my imagination."

Grace was mourning not only David's passing, but also her inability to tell her friends and family about this phenomenon. The few times she had tried, she told me, they had smiled and looked at her as if she were daft. "I won't do that again," she stated.

Instead, she came to see me. While she was embarrassed and chagrined to be talking to a psychic and medium, she was relieved to have someone believe her sightings of her dead husband.

"It is not at all uncommon," I told her. "As a matter of fact, over half of the spouses of deceased partners experience some sort of contact with the deceased in the first year."

"What do they do then?" asked Grace, her face momentarily lighting up.

"It is really up to you, Grace," I told her. "You can pretend that it didn't happen and soon enough he will go away. Or, you can open yourself to that experience and learn to use your intuition to maintain contact, not only with him, but also with other guides and information that is available to you. David is giving you one last gift. He is giving you the gift of intuitive access and wisdom."

Over the twenty years or more that I have been a professional psychic and medium, I have heard hundreds of stories like that of Grace. The circumstances of the occurrence are very different from person to person, but the effect is the same. Something happens—a death perhaps, or a business failure or a significant illness—that prompts an awakening of sorts. They hear the still, small voice of intuitive knowing that has been lying dormant within them since childhood. They may have heard its call before, but this time they listen.

Very often these occurrences happen in the last third of a person's life. A number of factors come into play to make this so. First, older people are usually finished with the embracing, fulfilling, yet distracting times of child rearing and career development. Often, they have entered a period where they have the time and money to do some soul searching.

Also, the death of a spouse or child, the risk of a serious or life-threatening illness, or even the trauma of a midlife career or relationship change is much more common as we age. Not many of us escape our fifties without some sort of wake-up call from the spirit realm.

It is as if we are programmed to awaken our natural intuitive ability at this stage of our life. We are, in fact, invited by spirit into what I have coined "the elder generation." The purpose of this book is to help the reader join in this cultural and spiritual revival of elders, sages, crones, and wise ones.

Souls come into this world with most of their memories intact. They also come in fully connected to the world of spirit and the information it contains. They know that they are one with all beings, and that what one knows, we all know.

Until this knowledge is socialized out of them, children act on this knowing. Spend time with a small child and notice how alert they are to things you cannot see. Often they will have conversations with "imaginary" friends. They will stare at a corner, seemingly communicating with an unseen being. When they first begin to draw or color, they often draw what they see: bright vivid colors surrounding human bodies, floating balls of light, and doorways into other dimensions.

Of course, all too soon they are told to color between the lines, ignore the boogieman in the closet, and quit making things up. After a time, even the memories of those experiences fade or are relegated to the status of a cute story. Socialization occurs and memories of past lives are laughed at until they are no longer mentioned and soon forgotten. Because of this, most people lose their ability to focus and psychically "know" things by about the age of seven. But, as this book will show, there is another time of life when psychic ability once again becomes commonplace. That is the time when, due to a number of different factors having to do primarily with aging, our intuitive abilities return. It is the time, usually around age fifty, when many of us join the elder generation. Before that stage of life most people, myself included, are far too busy living our lives to pay much attention to anything outside of our immediate existence. The realm of spirit and intuitive knowing fades away during much of our youth and middle adulthood.

During our early and middle adult years we are distracted from listening to our inner voices, much less the voices of other realms. Family, work, and social commitments occupy all of our waking moments. Few of us have more than a few seconds of silence in our days. If an intuitive voice or impression were to be calling you, would you hear it over your cell phones, iPods, and e-mails?

At midlife, however, an interesting thing happens. Most people experience something that prompts their inherent and yet forgotten intuitive abilities to resurface. My own wake-up call to intuitive knowing came via a perforated esophagus and a near-death experience. Yours may come due to a health issue, the death of a child or a spouse, or simply by coming face to face with the inevitability of mortality. Whatever the cause, most people experience a time when the veil between the world of spirit and that of flesh once again becomes permeable.

While sometimes happening at a younger age, it is generally around fifty that we begin inevitably to feel the call of spirit. For some it may come spontaneously, as when a widow suddenly feels the presence of her deceased husband or an illness prompts a near-death experience. While these trigger experiences become more and more common after the age of fifty, they can happen at any time of one's life. What is unusual about the individuals at this point, however, is that they are much more likely to heed the call and to act on what they are told or experiencing.

For some aging adults, this phenomenon may happen more slowly. They may find themselves becoming fascinated with inner work. There may be a strong urge to explore meditation, religious practices, or spiritual development in a way not felt before. As we age we all enter, in one way or another, that elder generation I spoke of. What we do then is the subject of this book.

Many of us are discovering that the things we desired and strived for when we were young no longer seem to matter as much. Before joining the elder generation, some of us first have a stereotypical midlife crisis. But soon, the affairs or Harleys or facelifts don't matter much either. Eventually, all of our life journeys inevitably lead us (sometimes kicking and screaming) face to face with the realm of spirit. No matter what event causes us to reach that point, once we do, we cannot go back.

How do you know when you have entered the elder generation?

While everyone is different, there are unifying factors. Ask yourself these questions:

1. Have you recently experienced a trauma, change, death, or illness that has caused you to think about life and death issues?

2. Do you find that the day-to-day business of life (i.e., work, home, shopping) no longer holds your full interest?

3. Have you noticed that you have difficulty explaining what you are feeling, especially to people younger than you?

4. Do you long for more time alone? Are people suggesting that you are becoming too solitary?

5. Are you sleeping more (or less) and having more vivid dreams?

6. Do you read the obituaries on a regular basis, not looking for people you know but rather out of curiosity as to how they lived and died?

7. Are you more interested in books, television programs, and films that have a spiritual nature than you used to be?

8. Do you find yourself acting upon your inner knowing with more frequency?

9. And, the most important factor: Are you nearing or over age fifty?

There is no scoring to this test. You will know within your innermost soul if you are part of the elder generation. I would certainly suspect that your very reading to this point is proof of your eligibility.

As we age, we have only two choices. We can embrace our natural human intuitive ability or we can deny it. In most cultures prior to the twentieth century, the aged were revered as wise ones who could see beyond the veil. The shamans, crones, midwives, and medicine men were generally aged persons who had lived long enough to master intuitive and mediumship skills. In a culture where living to old age was rare, those who were blessed in that fashion were honored and listened to for guidance.

With the advent of the industrial revolution and the dissolution of the extended family, older adults have become invisible and unimportant. However, that is about to change. One reason is that we now have a huge aging population. As of July 2, 2005, the US Census Bureau estimated there were 78.2 million baby boomers in the United States. In the year 2006, 7,918 people turned age sixty each day. We are hardly alone.

Like it or not, the baby boomers have changed society. As they now enter the elder generation, I believe that their awakening psychic powers will once again rock the world. We have the potential to be a huge force in our society. We dare not turn our backs on this resource.

In my consultations with people from all walks of life, one theme keeps recurring: as people age, they become more and more psychic. Some report spontaneous psychic occurrences that prompted them to explore this topic. Some people talk about being kicked in the pants by the spirit realm. It seems that the brain often compensates for decreasing memory and other cognitive skills by enhancing intuitive ability. It also appears that the lifestyles of older people allow for more quiet, solitude, and introspective time. Finally, the trials and tribulations that come with a full life will often trigger previously unnoticed psychic ability.

This book chronicles some of those stories. My hope is that you will recognize your own journey in the stories and take comfort in knowing you are not alone. I also give you some very concrete and specific tools with which to cultivate your new skill.

Being a part of the elder generation is the greatest gift we have yet to receive in this lifetime. We are being shown glimpses of our lives to come. We are being given information that we can use to help ourselves and those who follow us.

As the population bulge of the baby boomers morphs into the elder generation, we do so with the hope for peace and love that we started with in the 1960s. This time, however, we have more tools. We have experience, wisdom, psychic ability, and yes, money.

We can make a difference.

As we age we have a choice. We can become the shamans, crones, and wise people for our world. Or, we can live in the shadow of fear of aging and death. We can fade into an invisible generation, or we can step forward as the elder generation. We can embrace our ability to see beyond the veil or we can live in fear of passing to a place we do not know and of which we are terrified. The choice is ours to make.

In the end, we will pass from this world. How we live now is all that matters. This book is about embracing who we are in joy and soulfulness. It is about claiming our place as wisdom seers. Join me then, as part of the elder generation.

one

....

My Story

Most cultures and religions have some belief in an afterlife. It is part of the human condition, it seems, to believe, indeed to *know*, that we are eternal beings. While many, if not most, people believe in an afterlife, few have even considered that there is also a before life.

We are, in fact, eternal souls who live for a short time in a human body. Our souls have memories, not only of this lifetime but also of our existence between lives, and of other lifetimes in other bodies. Even while on earth, we have direct access to information from the realm of spirit.

Many people will, of course, disagree with the above premises. There have been and will always be arguments and discussions about the nature of life and death, and what comes before and after. I will leave that discussion for the philosophers, critics, pundits, and academics, for I know that we live forever.

I know this, not only because I have I experienced my own vivid memories of past lives and times between lives, but also because I talk to spirits of deceased persons on a regular basis. While most children rather quickly forget their past lives and memories, some do not. I was one of those. In my case, I believe a variety of factors contributed to my unique ability to remember the spirit realm and continue to converse with it.

I was an "instrument baby," pulled so violently from the womb that my head still does not grow hair in a large spot where the forceps bruised me—I was wrenched into this existence.

I vividly remember the experience. It *hurt,* and the lights were too bright, the smells overwhelming. My parents always laughed when I insisted that I remembered being born, even though I could describe it with great accuracy.

With an oblong head and a blue face, I was not a beautiful newborn. Somehow I knew from birth that I would never be quite like everyone else.

I was a sickly child, allergic to almost everything and severely asthmatic. Back in the 1950s, asthmatic children weren't allowed to run and play like other children. I spent my days resting on a couch while watching a grainy black and white television or reading voraciously. Movement exacerbated my symptoms, so I was excused from all physical activity. I missed most of the first grade because I was too sick to tolerate a full day of school. I spent my nights propped up in a sitting position because I couldn't breathe while lying down.

I was exceedingly shy and quiet and, because I couldn't play like other children, I had very few friends. But I was not lonely; I had lots of spirits to talk to and things to learn.

In the tiny Minnesota town of Hinckley where I grew up, intuitive knowing was considered suspect, sinful, or just plain crazy. And I was, by all accounts, a strange kid. I couldn't ride a bike, throw a ball, or run. I had no interest in dolls or toys. I taught myself to read around four years of age and spent all of my time with my face in a book, as my mother would say. I also developed an unexplainable fascination with people's hands. By the time I was four or five years old, I had discovered that I could learn about a person by looking at their palm. The lines, particularly those in the hands of my grandmother's elderly friends, fascinated me. "Look," I would say to them while pointing to a line, "this is when you got married, and these are your children." I was surprised that they couldn't see what to me was in plain sight.

I didn't have a clue as to what I was doing, and for a time people thought it was cute. Then they decided it was just plain spooky, and I was told to quit. However, by that time I was hooked. I asked our local librarian for books on palmistry. I learned the names of the lines and the standard interpretations. Then I decided what was true based on my innermost knowing. Kids at school would let me practice on them—until their parents found out. I also learned that I could "sneak peeks" at people's hands when they weren't looking, and, finally, I learned that I could sometimes know all I wanted just by turning my attention toward the person, even if I couldn't see the hands.

In retrospect, I believe that my self-taught intuitive training was invaluable. Because of my illness (and weirdness), I was left pretty much alone. I was quiet enough that people generally ignored me, which was usually all right with me. I would study them, figuring out their stories, making up their histories. It was a hobby I could do without much movement or companionship. I now believe I was lucky. I was not socialized out of my psychic ability.

Then, when I turned twelve years of age, my asthma mysteriously disappeared. I spent many years thereafter attempting to be normal and ignoring my psychic skills.

As my health was restored, the veil between the spiritual and physical worlds turned into a solid, locked door. I worked very hard to think and act like my peers. I wanted more than anything else to do the things that other people did. I wanted to be able to do physical activities and play sports. I yearned to be popular and to go on dates. I dreamed of getting married and having a career.

What I did not want to be was a mystic. For once, I was determined to fit in. For a few years I used palmistry as a party game. Then, in an effort to conform to the world, I consciously attempted to forget the visions and the gifts.

I spent nearly twenty years on my quest for normalcy. During that time I finished college, where I majored in psychology and sociology. I married a kind, gentle, and very normal man, and together we bought a split-level house in an average suburb. On the outside, I seemed to have accomplished my goal; I was as middle American as you could get.

On the inside, I still felt like a freak. I would awaken with the awful feeling that I'd forgotten to do something terribly important. My dreams were full of symbolism, deadlines missed, unkept promises. I worked at that time as a probation officer, interviewing convicted felons and writing reports about their history and crime for the court. I was very good at it. Without asking, I knew their innermost fears and their motivations. But the quiet voice of intuition nagged at me.

I may have heard it, but I chose to ignore it. Like nearly everyone else, my goals were far more practical: a house, a family, a career.

As I neared the age of thirty, I wondered. "What could I do that would make me feel confident and self-assured?" I looked around the courthouse where I worked and saw a group of people who seemed fearless. I wanted to be like them—so I went to law school.

Soon, I was able to lose myself in a sea of contracts and torts. I still worked full-time as a probation officer while attending law school four nights a week. Weekends were devoted to studying. There was no time for things of the spirit, nor any time for introspection. I learned that staying very busy quiets the nagging voice of intuition. In fact, if your life pace is frantic enough, that whisper may even become inaudible for a time. I would soon learn that ignoring the voice would cause it to return with a shout.

Six weeks prior to my graduation from law school, my life took an irrevocable turn. My husband and I were having a rare meal at home together when I felt a sudden and intense pain in my chest. Unable to trace a cause, I waited until the pain was unbearable before he rushed me screaming to the emergency room.

My esophagus had perforated without warning. I had suffered from swallowing difficulties since I was a child but had always been told it was due to "nerves." It would later be discovered that I had a condition known as Barrett's esophagus, which caused ulcer-like sores to gradually eat holes through tissue. But that night, my condition did not appear serious enough to get the attention it truly deserved. We were met in the emergency room by a bored intern who instructed me to swallow malt-sized cups of barium for X-rays of my digestive tract. Unable to find the obstruction he antici- pated, he inserted a nasogastric (NG) tube down my nose, gave me a shot of Demerol, checked me into a hospital bed, and returned to his crossword puzzle.

The next morning, my chest cavity had filled with air, hardened barium, and an infection. I looked as if I had been injected with helium. Amazingly, the staff didn't appear to notice. I was placed in a wheelchair and taken to a clinic nearby.

The esophageal specialist turned pale the minute he saw me. He rushed from the room and came back a few minutes later with a chest surgeon. I knew, from the look of panic on their faces, that something was terribly wrong.

Wishing to consult privately, they wheeled me into a small storage room adjacent to the examining room. I sat in the wheelchair and felt my life force weaken. Suddenly, I noticed that I was observing the room from a different perspective. Everything was much clearer and brighter. Although I didn't have my glasses on, I could see with a vividness I had never before experienced.

I looked down to see a rather pathetic sight. My body was scrunched down in the wheelchair, no longer able to support itself upright. It looked gray, very sick, very sad, and very pitiful. I realized with some surprise that that was me. I also realized I was dying. And I discovered that I didn't care. I had no more attachment to that body than I would have to a pair of discarded and worn-out shoes.

Leaving my body behind, I departed the room. While traveling near ceiling level, I proceeded to the area where the two doctors were consulting frantically. I could tell they were alarmed by my condition. I watched impassively as they desperately discussed various options for my care. The emergency room doctor, they feared, had totally misdiagnosed my condition. They were concerned that he might have inserted the NG tube through the hole in my esophagus and into my chest rather than down into my stomach. The barium that I had swallowed the night before had escaped into my chest cavity, where it had hardened overnight into a cement-like substance that encased some of my internal organs.

I listened to their conversation without alarm. I knew that if they didn't do something immediately, the body in the other room would die. I also knew with certainty that it simply did not matter. I have never felt such peace.

The next day, I awoke in the recovery room after emergency chest and stomach surgery. The doctors had saved my life.

I spent the last six weeks of my law school term in the intensive care unit. Although I was allowed to graduate with my class, I never returned to the school. The perforated esophagus that had almost taken my life would change my life in ways I would not fully appreciate until years of pain, frustration, addiction, and despair had passed.

Until the day my esophagus perforated, I had spent my life striving for the future. Vacations, family, hobbies, everything I allegedly valued had been delayed for the sake of my goal to be a lawyer. I had always believed that someday it would all pay off and I would have the time and money to make up for all the delayed pleasures. Then, without any warning, I found myself lying in a hospital bed while feeding tubes pumped in nutrients, antibiotics, and painkillers, and chest tubes pumped out toxins and infection. My goal then became surviving until the next shot of morphine. My biggest achievement was the day I was able to sit up by myself.

After six weeks in the hospital, I returned home to study for the bar examination. Amazingly, I passed the test with flying colors. Despite my illness, my husband and I set up a law practice near our home. On the surface, I had not only survived, I had accomplished all of my goals. But none of them seemed very important anymore. Becoming a lawyer had been a goal I had strived toward for four long years—perhaps all my life. I had lived my life on a timetable with the unwavering belief that if I worked hard, studied hard, and saved money, I would somehow achieve that nameless, faceless calling that haunted me in those rare quiet moments when I actually stopped working.

In the five years that followed my hospitalization, I struggled to recover from my illness, two chest and stomach surgeries, and my subsequent addiction to painkillers. I was able to focus on little but the pain. I knew that I had changed, but I didn't know how. Nothing was important anymore. I'd become a lawyer. It was a good job, but I knew it wasn't my calling. It was how I made my living, not how I lived. How could I be proud of becoming a lawyer when I now knew that life was tenuous at best? I had faced death squarely and seen that nothing mattered. But where did I go from there? My wake-up call to the realm of spirit had come early.

Gradually, as the pain became manageable and narcotics dropped their hold on my soul, I reentered life. But I wasn't the same person. I developed an overriding passion to experience the world. I changed from being a woman who had barely left the state of Minnesota to a person who spent much of her disposable cash and time traveling the world. I felt driven to see and to do things that I'd previously had no interest in experiencing.

I had lived when I should have died and would never look at life the same again. My near-death experience caused a life metamorphosis that left me with different values, ideas, and a heightened sense of mystery and intuition. I could no longer deny who or what I was. I could no longer pretend the gifts I had been given were valueless. I entered upon a lifelong quest for myself. These feelings of different values, emerging intuition, and a sense of not fitting in and restlessness are all hallmarks of the elder generation as well.

As soon as I started using my intuitive gifts again, my life changed. I no longer wondered what I had forgotten; I knew what I was to do. You will find, I hope, that same feeling of relief as you read this book. By embracing our intuitive gifts, we once again become whole people who use our entire brain. Ten years after starting my law firm, I began teaching and training on intuitive development. As a practicing attorney with a successful firm in a small conservative suburb of Minneapolis, I was a little concerned about what teaching intuition classes would do to my reputation. Still, I had come out of the closet a few years before with the publication of my first book on palmistry. Once you've been billed as the "palm-reading lawyer" on television, print, and radio, teaching intuition looks almost reputable. Even though I knew that the acceptance and interest in intuition in our society was changing, I was still surprised at the reception given to my training programs. Within a few months of offering my first class, I was being called to train police, teachers, secretaries, correction workers, and business and professional people. Many in these groups were skeptical, but all were curious. We have reached a point where we know, at a deep inner level, that it is time to reclaim our intuitive heritage.

Because of my background in corrections and law, I found a unique niche in the training field. Shortly after I started teaching intuitive techniques, I was asked to train police officers how to use and trust their "blue sense." For several years I trained all the rookie officers of the St. Paul, Minnesota, police force, and also worked with many other jurisdictions, corrections officers, and security forces.

Police are a challenging group to train. While intuition (what they call blue sense) is highly valued and utilized by all successful officers, they are also suspicious of anything metaphysical. My job was to prove to them that not only did intuition exist, but that it was practical and useful. During one of my training programs I was certain I had finally done something that would get me fired. It was my first chance to train police officers in intuitive techniques, and from the looks of it, it might also be my last. Shortly into an exercise using psychometry (a technique of holding objects while getting intuitive information from them), a young male officer was slumped down in his chair while being fanned with a piece of paper by his partner. "What had happened to him that could create such a reaction?" I wondered.

The officer did look as if he might pass out at any moment. His face was ashen as he told the tale. I had asked each officer to partner up with someone they did not know well. They were to exchange personal objects such as rings or watches and then use their intuition to *read* impressions about the other person or object. I had chosen to do this exercise early in their training, primarily to get them out of their analytical mode of thinking. I hadn't expected great things at this stage but hoped to break down some of the skepticism and doubt that had met me a few hours before when I walked into the training room.

The shaken officer had been one of the most skeptical of the lot. He had the build of a young man who spent a lot of time lifting weights and working out. During my initial description of intuition, I had read a lot of doubt, even hostility, in his expression. Now, he looked confused and more than a little frightened. His partner for the exercise, a petite blond with her hair pulled back severely into a bun, appeared to be more excited than fearful. She looked slightly dazed as they told the class what happened.

Officer Mike started. "I have to admit that I thought this whole thing was a bunch of hooey. I never would have done this if it wasn't required," he said. "So, I wasn't expecting anything when I gave Susan my car keys. She held them for a minute and then she told me about a near accident my family and I were in a couple of years ago." He hesitated and then whispered softly, "But the weird thing is, she knew all about it—she saw the mountain road—even knew it was Colorado. She told me about the van, and how we'd just barely avoided going off a cliff!" He paused again. "She couldn't have known that—it's impossible."

Susan looked up. "I didn't—honest!" She seemed afraid I would accuse her of cheating somehow. "I only met Mike a few months ago when we entered police training together here in Minnesota. We're not really good friends—I didn't even know he'd been to Colorado."

"It was a vacation," Mike interjected. "You couldn't have known. I'm sure I haven't told that story to anyone here. It was a long time ago, and nobody got hurt or anything."

By this time, the class of forty or fifty police trainees was fascinated. I could hear murmurs around the room. "How did she do that?" "What did it feel like?" "It must have been a coincidence." "He had to have told her something."

The rest of the day went well, although without any more dramatic occurrences. After class, Susan stopped to talk to me. "What do I do now?" she asked. "How do I live my life knowing that I can do this?" A better question, I told her was this: "How could you live your life *not* knowing you could do this?" Susan had just discovered her gift, a gift we all have. But, unless Susan continued to use this gift, it would be filed away. Often it only emerges as we age and slow down. Susan had a choice: she could ignore this gift and pretend it never happened, or she could study and practice and turn it into a tool that she could use in conjunction with her logical, analytical brain to turn her into the best police officer (and human being) that she was capable of being. The choice was up to her.

Many of us have had that choice as well, but we have chosen to ignore it and just live our lives. Then, as we enter the elder generation, the gift comes back with a vengeance. Scientists tell us that in fact we only use 1.5 percent of our brain's ability. The rest, I believe, is there waiting to be tapped when we evolve into a species able to handle all the magnificent power of our bodies, minds, and spirits with integrity and intent. It takes a certain level of maturity and perspective to handle the power of being psychic. Perhaps this is another reason that so many of us wait until midlife or later to develop our intuitive ability.

One of the best uses of intuition was told to me during a training program I was conducting for graduates of the FBI national academy. Martin was one of the attendees. A career police officer, he had been on the force of a major metropolitan police department for nearly thirty years.

When I asked the audience to volunteer intuitive stories, there was a long period of silence. No one wanted to be the first to admit that something "spooky" had happened to him or her. Finally, a voice came from the back of the room. "Ask Martin about the missing girl," it said.

Everyone's eyes turned to Martin. He squirmed slightly and then told a tale that was infamous in police circles. "Several years ago," he began, "I was an investigator for our missing persons division. We got a call about an eight-year-old girl who had been missing for several days. The last time she'd been seen was when she and some friends were playing at a construction site south of town. When she didn't come home that night, her parents and their friends searched the site thoroughly, as did the local officers the next day. Nothing showed up; she had disappeared without a trace.

"By the time our department was called in, all possible evidence had been erased by a heavy snowfall and further construction work. Nonetheless, we spent all day combing the site," he went on. "There was nothing to give us a clue to her whereabouts.

"I went home that evening, but I simply couldn't relax," Martin continued. "I just knew she was at that site. Finally, I returned to the area by myself. It was dark and cold as I wandered around aimlessly. I kept going back to a particular place. I know it sounds crazy but it felt as if I was being called to a certain spot. I just stood there waiting in the dark and the quiet—and then I heard a faint cry, coming from directly below me!"

Martin continued his story as the room grew hushed. "I was standing directly on top of her," he whispered. "She had crawled into a hole, and a piece of heavy sheet metal had fallen over the top. Then snowfall had completely covered all signs of the opening. She'd been there for three days. I would never have heard such a weak call if I hadn't been standing immediately above her!"

Martin was uncomfortable with calling this an intuitive event. He did admit it was a remarkable coincidence or case of synchronicity. He also said he was more than a little bit tired of being teased about becoming the department psychic. "It was just a fluke," he said. "I'm really happy we found that girl. But I sure don't want to do that again. It's just too weird for me!"

Without intending to do so, Martin had used many of the elements of intuition, and, by doing so, he had saved a life. My hope is that, by reading this book and recognizing yourself in some of the stories, you, too, will learn to listen to and trust your own emerging intuition. In these pages, you will read the stories of dozens of people who have had their lives transformed. Some of the changes were dramatic, like my own; others were more of a gentle awakening. All of them have one thing in common. After experiencing a life change through some happening or process, all the writers committed to a journey of soul exploration and psychic development. They studied, meditated, and changed so that they could not only live fuller lives, but also be of benefit to society. I hope these stories enrich you and inspire you to do the same.

It was my illness that caused me to challenge the very premises on which I defined my life. I was thirty years old at the time. For most people, these challenges do not occur until much later in life. I was, I now see in retrospect, joining the elder generation at an early age. Since regaining my health in the 1980s, I have dedicated my life to honing and controlling my psychic ability. I was no longer content to have intuition be something that happened to me. I wanted it to be an accessible, controllable, and usable skill I could call upon at my command. Over the years I have trained thousands of people to trust in and utilize their psychic ability. Most of them were at midlife and beyond. It is the time of life when people have the time, resources, and interest in fostering theses gifts. As you read these pages and the many stories of people whose psychic ability has emerged, I believe you will also wish to join this community of powerful elders, shamans, and wise persons.

two

....

If We Were Born Psychic, How Did We Lose It?

Part of the way I gathered stories for this book was by placing a questionnaire on my website (see appendix). I was very pleased by the volume of responses I received from all over the United States. It was obvious that the idea of the elder generation resonated with a large group of people.

Of course, this was hardly a scientific survey. I have, quite honestly, very little interest in statistics or science and will leave those issues for someone who does. The people who responded were clearly people who were already interested in psychic phenomena. But that is the point, is it not?

One of the questions I asked in my survey was "At what age did you first feel that you had psychic ability?" A large majority of respondents answered that they had first become aware of their ability when they were young children. As we have discussed earlier, however, people seem to lose this ability, or at least turn it off, by about the age of seven. There are many reasons for that, of course. The following stories explain, at least partially, why this happens.

Children don't think psychic experiences (or any experiences for that matter) are unusual until someone tells them that they are. Over and over I heard something like this: "It probably started as a child, but I didn't think much of it, assuming everyone was like that."

Shelly describes it well: "When I was probably six or seven years old, I was remote viewing (a form of seeing without the use of our physical eyes) without knowing what I was doing. I would *see* through the eyes of animals, for example. I loved the outdoors and it was my haven. I was very sensitive to people around me and was extremely prone to headaches that were medically unexplained. Looking back, I would say with confidence that my headaches were due to the issue of sensitivity. I also never had a desire to have many friends throughout my youth. I found groups to be taxing on me. The usual peer dynamics of elementary school-aged girls was of no interest to me. I truly did not understand what it was they were doing together or why. I tried to fit in but found it too exhausting.

"Then, in my young adult years everything psychic turned off except for my being the pillar of advice for many friends for years. I could give them advice and forecast things without knowing what I was doing. All I knew was I helped many friends through difficult times."

Shelly's story is a good example of how psychic ability works in young children. Because they don't know that they can't do things (like see through the eyes of animals) they are able to do so. Many times though, they feel it cuts them off from their peers and family. Often, they even develop physical issues (such as Shelly's headaches or my asthma). As children age, the world laughs at them when they tell psychic tales and tells them it is impossible. And so, the ability goes away.

John wrote that he was telepathic with his mother from age eight to fifteen. In adolescence, he says, it went away. It took what John terms a midlife crisis at around age forty to prompt him to study all forms of psychic phenomena and to ultimately become a healer and practicing psychic.

Pam describes her early psychic experiences wonderfully. She says, "I felt it early on. I couldn't figure out why people were always telling lies and no one noticed. It was confusing.

"I also remember being confused by the teacher's asking, 'What kind of day is this?' and then pointing to a picture of a cloudy day. I would think, 'No, it isn't. It is a blue day or a magenta day.' I really loved magenta days."

Pam continues: "I also had 'imaginary' friends who were around a lot. I spent a lot of time alone. I talked to spirits of the dead, and some playful spirits. Always my imagination, I was told."

Like Pam, most children are told it is their imagination and are talked out of having "magenta days." They are often ridiculed, shunned, and told they are making things up. Very soon, usually around age seven, most children shut it out of their conscious awareness. There it stays, in our unconscious, speaking to us only in dreams, and waiting for us to get around to paying attention to it again.

Sometimes, our very beliefs and religious upbringing cause us to turn our back on our psychic abilities. Mary describes what happened to her at a very young age: "I had my tonsils and adenoids removed. A few days after returning home, I nearly bled to death, due to complications. A little girl about my age stayed with me the entire time. She was very sweet and kind. I floated out of my parents' bedroom while the doctor was trying to help me. (In those days, the doctor came to the home of his patients.) I watched my mother crying in the living room. My grandmother was with her and was trying to calm her.

"Later, I was on complete bed rest for days, due to the amount of blood I had lost. I told my mother and grandmother about the little girl who stayed with me. They asked me to describe her. I described her right down to the dress she was wearing. It turns out I had perfectly described a cousin of mine who had passed away at age three, when I was an infant. The dress I described was the dress that she had been buried in."

Mary continues with her story: "I believe that my cousin wanted my mother and grandmother to know that she had been with me while I was in such danger. By the way I described her, they were able to know it was her, and that she had been with me. Imagine the shock my mother and grandmother had when I told them I had seen them in the living room during my ordeal. I saw them while floating over them. I told it to them exactly the way it was."

Why didn't Mary retain this ability throughout her life? As she says, "Having been raised a Catholic and having gone to a strict Catholic school, I thought this was a bad thing. When anything unusual happened, I kept it to myself, except that often times I would tell my mother, and then my husband, as I got older."

Susan describes how she was able to hear and see spirits and other beings from a very young age. Instead of being comforting though, she found it very frightening. She says, "Growing up in an old farmhouse was frightening for me. We moved there from the city when I was four years old. Our family used to hear doors slamming, keys in locks, glass breaking, and wagons crossing the field at night. We could never explain what it was. We didn't think anything of it until we figured out that the slamming door was nailed shut, there was no broken glass, nobody was downstairs moving the chairs, and so on. We couldn't do anything about it so we ignored it, and I think it went away."

She goes on to say: "From this experience in my life I always knew there was so much more going on that people weren't aware of or not paying attention to."

As an adult, Susan continued to have psychic experiences, but again, ignored or put them aside. As a young mother, she wrote: "We were living in the country, sheltered from city life. We had five children and I was alone with them most nights. I had been reading books about Edgar Cayce (a 1930s psychic and prophet) and things were happening. I felt a presence in our home. One morning I found our newborn on the floor. A few days later my husband said he found a baby horse's head in our yard. It was scary for me. I quit reading about psychic abilities and took a bible study course instead. I felt a little safer but I was still afraid. I remember a dream that was an invitation that was beautiful, where I was offered a powerful voice that entered my being in a golden spiral as my friends were watching me. I pushed it away and trembled in fear for weeks."

It is no wonder that, having had such experiences, Susan pushed away her innate psychic abilities. It was another twenty years before she learned how to use them and felt comfortable with them. She continues: "My interest and courage returned twenty years later. The voice [she had heard in her dream] returned and I am now using it, singing and channeling."

Now, Susan says, "I studied energy healing and medicinal herbs. I had a sense of gratitude and love for the plants that I used, I felt a need to honor and repay them so I sang to them. I was surprised to hear the beautiful voice and songs that weren't mine. I continue to use that voice to clear homes and heal sometimes. Most often I sing to myself after being with people. It's always a different song. That started happening shortly after I turned fifty."

Susan took what were terrifying experiences in earlier life and turned them into comforting and healing powers that she uses for her own and other's benefit. As with so many of us, she found the courage to do that as part of her entry into the elder generation.

As these stories illustrate, it is not that we are unable to re-awaken our intuition earlier than our forties or fifties. It is just that it usually takes that long to find the time and inclination.

However, many of the people who answered my survey told of psychic happenings at earlier times in their lives. Some of them are quite dramatic. For example, Sheryl tells of "an awe-inspiring experience of a Oneness with the Eternal at age fifteen that I could not explain." She never forgot it, she says, but she also never talked about it.

Kathleen wrote saying she had been intuitive since she was three and had never lost that ability. As she put it, "I have pretty much experienced psychic things all my life. It is a part of my soul. I am frequently told where my keys are and 'did you remember to shut off the water?' 'Please be careful, slow down, there is a squad car checking speeds just up the road.' These are a part of my life, and I do not feel like a freak. Quite actually, I believe I am the wave of the future, living in both worlds."

Kathleen was able to keep her innate psychic ability with her throughout her adult years. That is rare, though. Usually, we tuck it far away and forget about it—until we get our psychic wake-up call. Often, it takes an emergency to break through the barrier we put around our psychic knowing as we become adults. Sometimes psychic information breaks through this wall to warn us of something. For example, Kris tells of an incident in 1975. She says, "I was pregnant at the time and had a two-year-old child. A light bulb burned out in my home and I sensed that something about the burnt-out bulb was not right. I felt the ceiling and it seemed warm to me.

"I called the fire department just to check it out. By the time they arrived there was a major fire going. The firefighter told me that if I had ignored it and gone to bed, my daughter and I would have been dead in a few hours from the fire. He wanted to know what made me know there was something wrong. I could not explain it then and still cannot. I just know someone was watching over us."

Psychic ability does not always show itself through signs from spirits or warnings of life-threatening events. Much of the time, actually, we get small messages.

Barb tells of how at age sixteen, she "was going to meet my girlfriend, who had just gotten home from Europe. As I was walking down the street, I had a vision of a string bag, which is a type of shopping bag. When we met for lunch, she handed one to me that she had brought back as a gift for me. It was identical to the one I had envisioned."

Steve tells of how, in his twenties, he discovered his psychic ability by playing bridge. He always seemed to know, he says, what cards his partner and opponents were holding.

If we have this sort of ability all of our lives, why don't we use it more often? As Lisa says, "I was so afraid of it (psychic ability) in my twenties that I made a conscious effort to stifle events and feelings. Now that I am in my forties, I wish I could relive some of those events because they were so unbelievable. I feel like I cannot remove the wall I put up to block out things, but I want to because I am so interested again and feel that I can handle it now."

Fear is a major reason why we block our psychic ability in our youth and mid-years. During those years we are raising a family and fostering our careers. We don't want to be ridiculed or laughed at. We don't want to seem like we are airy-fairy or crazy. And we certainly don't wish to fool around with anything that might be dangerous for us or our family.

Perhaps one of the hallmarks of those of us in this midlife stage is just this; we no longer care as much about what others think about us. We have the courage to dust off intuitive skills we have kept hidden...even from ourselves. And we have the time and the interest to learn how to tear down the walls we have put up to keep us from our inner knowing.

My niece, who is thirty-seven, is a nurse anesthesiologist working in the emergency room of a busy Minneapolis hospital. She is married, lives in a lovely, large house, and has three beautiful daughters, ages one, two, and four. She is also a whirling dervish of activity. Her life is full of family, work, and social obligations. She has no time for whispers from the intuitive realm.

Most people her age have lives very similar to that. It seems there are two times in our lives when we have the time and inclination to listen to our psychic whispers...when we are young and when we are aging.

We live in the best of all times to be aging. With life expectancies approaching eighty, many of us have plenty of time, and lots of quiet and even leisure, to examine, cultivate, and nurture our intuition. First, though, we have to wake up.

....

three

What Does Aging REALLY Look Like?

We hear so much about the downsides of aging that it is often what we tend to focus on. As it turns out, however, study after study shows that older people are happier, calmer, and more content that younger people. This makes sense. As our intuitive abilities increase and we trust and use them more, our lives get easier and better.

In January of 2009, *Real Simple* magazine surveyed 2,600 people about their happiness. They found that 55 percent of women in their sixties described themselves as being "very happy." This was compared to just 40 percent of women in their twenties. Other more scientific studies have found the same thing. *ScienceDaily* (May 19, 2008) states, "Aging brings a sense of peace and calm." A new study from the Population Research Center at the University of Texas at Austin found that, "starting at about age sixty, participants reported more feelings of ease and contentment than their younger counterparts."

There are many reasons for this. We are, after all, at a time in our lives when most of us are free, generally healthy, and relatively well off. More than that, though, we literally view the world with different eyes.

ScienceDaily.com reports that "Medical researchers have identified brain activity that causes older adults to remember fewer negative events than their younger counterparts. Neuroscientists from Duke University Medical Center have discovered that older people use their brains differently than younger people when it comes to storing memories, particularly those associated with negative emotions."

Another study done at the University of Texas at Austin, partially funded by the National Institute of Aging, reached the same conclusion. Aging, the study found, is associated with more positive than negative emotions, and more passive than active emotions. Or, as I would put it, as we age we become happier, less driven by our emotions, and more intuitive. Being part of the elder generation is something to cheer about.

Some side effects of aging are having more peace, being comfortable in one's own skin, and being less driven by emotions. Lael, age fifty-nine, put it this way: "I am sleeping well every night. I meditate in the evening, and then am able to fall into a deep sleep every night. Even nights when I don't get to meditate, I still sleep very well." She went on to say: "I never expected these gifts to be mine and I am so happy to be on this journey."

Dee, age seventy, also described how she views this wonderful gift. She says, "In times of quiet meditation, I can feel the presence of loving and helpful spirits. I know that everything happens for a reason, and I am confident that I can hear what to do, and do it without worrying too much about it. I will ask a question prior to meditation or sleeping, and will soon get the answer AND I know it is right."

As we age, we also tend to become more comfortable in our own bodies. While society may worship at the feet of the young and beautiful, it is the elders who truly accept themselves. Rose, age sixty-four, describes it this way: "I am very comfortable being me, with gray hair, short fingernails, clothes that are comfortable, and loving my family, nature, and being me." Carolyn, age fifty-one, uses different words to describe self-acceptance. What she has, she says, is "a growing sense to just come home to who I am, and a restlessness of not wanting to try to fit in."

Sheryl, age fifty-four, tells of finding freedom from her old habit of self-criticism. She says, "I am happier, more at peace, loving what is, without my old habit of beating myself up. Great use of words, as I believe I have moved out of the victim archetype into a new core of self-confidence."

Consider Paula's words at age fifty-seven. She states: "Spirit got my attention in an amazing way when I was about fifty-three, and then I made a conscious decision to live consciously with spirit in a new, freer, fearless way."

Freer and fearless are words that kept popping up in the questionnaires and conversations I had about this topic. Being part of the elder generation is perhaps the freest time of a person's life. Developing psychic awareness allows for us to live in a free and fearless fashion that would have been impossible when we were younger.

In my own life, I have found that fear no longer rules me. This certainly was not always true for me. Maybe all children are fearful. I don't know. I just remember, as a little girl, being terrified a lot. Mostly, I was afraid of three things: nuclear war, Nazis, and the Rapture.

I was a child of the fifties, with a father who returned from World War II with a bullet in his knee and night terrors. In my nightmares, I hid from Nazis that searched for little girls in closets.

Then came the cold war. I was taught how to hide under my desk in school in case a nuclear bomb was launched. Even in college, I was certified as a bomb shelter manager.

But my biggest fear was the Rapture. For those of you lucky enough not to know that term, it is, according to fundamentalist Christians, the time when all the good Christian folk will be taken bodily up to heaven, before the Apocalypse starts for the rest of us sinners. I was only about five years old, but I was pretty sure I was not good enough to be "taken up." Whenever I was left alone, I was convinced that the rest of my family had ascended into heaven while I had been left behind to face the four horsemen.

Plus I was a sick little thing. Plagued with asthma, I never learned to run or play like normal kids. I read, watched a lot of matinee movies on television, and talked to the guides and spirits who take care of sickly kids like me.

Now I am telling this tale because I am not fearful anymore. One of the challenges of these latter years is that we need to have courage. It takes courage to predict things without proof. You need to be brave to stand up to the so-called skeptics. As I type this, I realize that I now *am* courageous. And I think to myself, "When did *that* happen? How did I get from being that terrified little girl to where I am today?"

Courage, sometimes, is feeling fear and doing what needs to be done anyhow. I am not sure we can rationally talk ourselves out of fear. Looking back, I am virtually certain I had nothing to fear from the Nazis. The bomb didn't drop on Hinckley, Minnesota. And if the Rapture occurred, it sure left a bunch of us still around.

As an adult, I finally figured out that none of those fears were even mine. Mostly, it was my parents' fears that I was picking up intuitively. My dad was the one who fought the Nazis. My mom was the person terrified of Hell. The media was pandering to my fear of bombs. The fear was not even mine, yet it crippled me for years.

So, in adulthood, I always ask when I feel fear: "Is this mine?" If I can't trace it to a real, concrete event in my life, it is probably NOT my fear and I can let it go.

If a car is bearing down at me and I am standing in the middle of the street, then fear is rational and will get me to jump. Other than that, fear seems to be mostly a mind killer. We, as members of the elder generation, no longer need to claim it as ours.

Even that biggest fear of all, death, loses much of its power over us. Terri (age fifty-five) states: "I no longer fear death. I value the little things more. I am happier. I have seen and heard spirits and beautiful singing voices sometimes when it rains."

The oldest of my respondents, JoAnn, at age eighty, wrote to wish me a joyous Easter season. Here is a quote from her that illustrates so beautifully how her trust in a spirit life also allows for a lack of fear of death: "I wish you joy and health and all the spring joys I can think of! All weeks are holy, but this one is named that... and so I wish you wholiness (I'm always coining words) this springtime of new life and hope... everywhere! Guess what I'm doing this week? I'm making funeral folders (readings/music/quotes/prayers) for both my husband and myself. No, we are not urgently terminal, in that sense, but we are getting along in years. I am eighty and Jim is a young eighty-one."

Wouldn't it be an amazing world if we could all, like JoAnn, look death merrily in the face as just another of life's transitions? Some of the side effects of aging intuitively are more peace of heart and a sense of well-being. Kay (forty-eight) describes it so well: "Nearing fifty, yes, I experience vivid happiness most of the time, a feeling of rightness, a loss of the anxiety and depression that has plagued me for some time." Leila describes it in different terms: "I have started getting these moments of peace where I am awed by the divine perfection of the world just the way it is. I have extreme gratitude for all of it."

Most of the elder generation find they need experiences more and things less. They also find a strong desire for solitude and nature. Kay (age forty-eight) says, "I feel a real kinship to animals, all animals. I am a person that will carry bugs outside or place them on my plants. The natural world is very comfortable for me. I feel at home where I am right now in my life." Dar (age fifty-three) puts it this way: "I have changed the way I think about prayer and meditation. Mine is more of a walking meditation and I thank my dog, Max, for that! That's where most of it seems to happen—out there on the road, under the sky, in the wind, with the earth crunching beneath my feet."

One of the myths about aging is that we are lonely. Perhaps that is true for some, but the members of the elder generation seldom mention that. We have the company of each other and spirits and guides. Plus, we like being alone. We are comfortable with ourselves and need far fewer things and people to occupy us.

Ann (forty-nine) describes her need to be alone to do her work: "Often, as I do my spiritual rituals, I am relieved that I am alone. How would anyone understand my deep need for privacy?"

Our definition of success often changes. Material things hold less value for the elder generation. As Laurie (forty-six) puts it, "Corporate American no longer fits. Having 'stuff' or shopping for 'stuff' seems silly or a waste of time/money/and energy." Maybe this is why our generation is so often ignored. Our spending power is amazing. According to the US Census Bureau (2007), American adults over fifty years of age have more than $1.5 trillion in discretionary spending dollars available, the highest disposable income of all age groups. We are just wise enough to know how to use it and what it can and cannot get us.

Our cravings become focused more toward the spiritual realm. We don't always know what we are looking for, but we know it is there for us to find. As Lisa (forty-eight) puts it, "I have an overwhelming desire, a nagging want, for something that I should be doing or knowing or learning. It is almost as if I have missed something and am being drawn to look into these things, but I do not know what it is."

Marie, at age seventy-five, is still feeling that way. She writes: "Right now, I seem to be on an almost driven path to learn more about and deepen my relationship with God. That may come from an experience of mortality upon reaching my seventy-fifth birthday. Why seventy-five was so significant, I've no idea—at this time. However, there is a reason lurking somewhere."

Carole (sixty-one) describes how she has changed since turning fifty: "I am very interested in anything spiritual. I read many books, meditate, pray, study Kabbalah, take classes, and lead a spiritual group of like-minded people. I also have successfully done automatic writing, journaling, etc."

Sheryl (fifty-four) describes it this way: "I surrendered to the universe's lessons, and opened myself to unknown experiences."

To younger people, it may seem that the elder generation is pulling away from the world. This is *not* true. The world is just as vivid for us, perhaps more so. We are just not as emotionally involved with it. Dar (fifty-four) explains it well: "I still get excited about world affairs but don't live in fear of world affairs, which is a new thing for me. I just know everything is going to be okay and watch it unfold." She goes on to say: "I do not feel isolated or different from others. I used to. Now I feel as though I belong to the community of me. And this is why I feel more and more comfortable with others and they are attracted to me."

Pam (fifty-two) describes this phenomenon well: "I am less likely to do something I really don't want to do (hopefully). I seem lazier. More dreamy than I was before if that is possible. I also feel less patient sometimes, but maybe I am just finally learning what the heck a boundary is."

As Pam so accurately puts it, one of the great gifts of being of this generation is that we have learned to set boundaries for ourselves. Our psychic gifts give us a lot of information about others, and our age gives us permission to know what to do with that knowledge.

Mary (fifty-eight) tells how just filling out the questionnaire helped her figure this out. She wrote, "Just making those checks was therapeutic! What an amazing feeling to have all the changes that niggle at me, or make me question what is going on with me, all in the same place. It gives me such a sense of comfort and relief. I have questioned my emotional maturity, because in recent years, being forced to deal with certain people (who I immediately and viscerally react to) can actually make me sick, and I just want to get away, avoid them at all costs, and I would ask myself, 'Why are you so weak that you let them affect you so much?' I see that in a different light after completing this questionnaire."

That is another great gift of our generation. As we talk about all of these changes and gifts, we become part of a community of elders, sages, and wise people.

Sometimes, the "pulling away" we do from the world is just that we have less judgment about it. As Wendy (fifty-one) describes it: "I'm much less judgmental and am much more open and able to be the observer of people and events. Things are happening much more synchronistically, and I'm amused and not at all surprised."

This is a commonly reported phenomenon. We lose our attachment to things and become, in some fashion, observers. We see and sense and feel things, but without the usual judgment that so much of the world seems to find necessary. Small things just don't matter as much anymore. Barb (fifty-six) describes it well: "I am aware of the space of time I may have left on earth. My husband and I are connecting on a higher plane; he has had a prostate cancer scare and we have focused on the quality of our life, and the incidentals don't matter as much. We are focusing on our retirement ideas, and are talking about future lifestyle choices."

Life simply gets better and easier when we trust and use our intuition. Joni (fifty-four) puts it well: "I have things pop into my head, it feels like thoughts or ideas, and I usually dismiss them only to find out that a few minutes to a few hours later I realize a reason that it popped into my head. I am now trying to pay more attention to my thoughts and knowing and acknowledge and act on them more quickly than before."

Mary tells of how her life dramatically improved after she tapped into her intuition at age fifty-three. "In late August and early September of 2008 several things happened all at once that were very amazing. My son left for college on a full ride with no college bills; my father-in-law died, appeared as a butterfly in my dreams, and left us money just as the economy was tanking; an old friend of my husband's died and left us money; I read Dr. Janis Amatuzio's books about people's experiences with spirits; I got a notice about a class on intuition, attended, and it was absolutely the best thing I ever did; I found out that one of my good friends has intuitive gifts. I reached a higher level of spirituality after these occurrences, and I am a different person now."

A better life is one of the gifts that comes naturally as intuition blossoms. Rita, at age seventy-two, describes her life this way: "I feel like I'm on a never-ending adventure as I discover new spiritual energies. I feel so much closer to all things spiritual and to my creator. I have so much joy in my heart and am truly at peace with death. I only wish I could have had the opportunity to learn about spiritual things when I was younger, but being brought up Catholic kept me from pursuing anything spiritual or 'super natural.' As I look back, I think my intuitiveness was awakened and working already when I was younger. I just didn't know it. This awakening has been such a gift to me at this point in my life."

If writing this book has taught me anything, it is that the natural progression and effects of aging are very different from what we are told by society and the media. I am struck by how wrong society's perception is of our generation. We are generally happy, at peace, our lives move smoothly, we trust our guides, we meditate and pray. We buy less and do more. We are freer than at any other time in our life. If there is a downside here, I don't see it.

four

Becoming an Elder

In October of 2008, I was privileged to travel to China for two weeks. One of the most delightful parts of that journey for me was to see the role of the elders in their society. In every park and garden in the country, elders gather to dance, exercise, and sing. The beauty of the orchestrated and graceful dances and tai chi exercise groups is difficult to describe. Most breathtaking of all, perhaps, was a day we spent at the Summer Palace listening to and enjoying the elders as they gathered in groups to sing and play music.

Our guide explained that in China, one became an elder at approximately age fifty-five (for women) to sixty (men). At that age, they effectively retired, and their days were then spent in the social gatherings I described. They received low-cost or free admission to the beautiful gardens or parks where they also gathered to play various games, talk, and just enjoy the beauty.

On occasion, you would see an elder taking care of a small child. Since, in China, each couple is only allowed to have one child, children are highly valued and called, jokingly, "little emperors." Even though almost all young people work outside the home in the new China, it did not seem that the elders were called upon to babysit, however. Rather, they were allowed to enjoy the company of the little ones when they chose. Traditional Chinese society expects adult children to care for their aging parents, not the other way around.

I joked that when I became an elder, I wanted to move to China. The guide looked at me in confusion, and I realized I already *was* an elder in his eyes.

Returning home and working on this book, I realized that the elder role I had observed in China was a model that fit in nicely with the premise of this book. (I realize that there are many horror stories of elder abuse in China as well. For the purpose of illustration, I am discussing only what I observed in my travels.)

Throughout much of recorded history, at least until the industrial revolution, elders had honored roles in Western society as well. Of course, most people died well before they were able to become elders. Those who survived into their fifties and beyond became the nurturers of the community, the spiritual leaders, the guardians of traditions, the teachers, mentors and initiators of the young. They were the storytellers who helped their people remember enduring wisdom. They were looked to for advice and counsel and were cared for by those who were younger.

Native societies have traditionally always honored their elders. An excellent example of this on the North American continent is found in the Iroquois Confederation. In those tribes, a prominent role of the elders was and is to ensure that tribal deliberations always consider the impact of decisions on the seventh generation to come.

Elders were and are honored members of Native tribes and are looked to with respect and given deference due to their years of accumulated knowledge and wisdom. Some become the shamans for their people. They see visions and prophesy.

In ancient Celtic times, aged women were called "crones." They also were revered as elders who embodied wisdom and earth knowledge. Crones cared for the dying and were spiritual midwives at the end of life, providing a link between this world and the next. They were teachers, healers, leaders, bearers of sacred power, knowers of mysteries, and walkers between the world of spirit and the world of substance. For thousands of years, older women were strong, powerful sources of wisdom and power. Crones were respected and honored in their communities.

The term "sage" was often used to describe the same role for an aged man. (Although this term now is used for both sexes.) A sage was and is a profoundly wise person, famed for experience and wisdom. As with the elders and crones, the requirement for being a sage was being a person of a certain age who had, through experience and wisdom, become a resource for leadership and knowledge for the community.

About the time of the industrial revolution, however, our society became a youth culture. Gradually, the honor and respect given to the elders eroded. The energy and vigor and new ideas of youth became valued, and the wisdom and vision of the elders was seen as irrelevant and outdated. Now, though, it is time for the elder generation to reclaim our position as advisors, mentors, shamans, and prophets.

During my recent group trip to Greece, the guide first called me "Mrs. Harwig." I was uncomfortable with that and told him to just call me Kathryn. For a while, he then called me "Mrs. Kathryn." I laughingly told him that didn't feel quite right either. Baffled, he asked what he could call me. (Because I was the group leader, he felt uncomfortable addressing me without a title.) I said, "Well, I suppose you could call me Queen Kathryn." After that, my group jokingly referred to me as the "Queen." I decided it rather fit.

As members of the elder generation, the characteristics of being a queen (or king) fit us better than many other choices we are handed, I believe. As it turns out, lots of midlife women are searching for an archetype to claim as their own. In our Pagan past, women were said to play three roles: the maiden, the mother, and the crone. These days though, not many of us like the idea of embracing the crone role. We envision being a crone as wizened, elderly, and powerless … the exact opposite of being a queen.

In times when a woman was likely to die during childbirth, it was rare to even reach menopause. Now, menopause and beyond occurs solidly in the middle of our lives. It is time to develop a new archetype for the post-motherhood years. And I am loving the idea of being a queen.

I believe that many women cling too long to the role of mother. Our thirty-year-old "children" are still living with many of us, playing too long the roles of "Maiden" and "Peter Pan." Even if we have no grown children in our homes, many of us continue to play the mother role in our jobs, with our spouses, and even with each other. Mothering is something we know how to do and it seems to come naturally to most of us.

We cling to being a mother partly, I suspect, because we have no other role open to us. Often, though, what we accomplish is not letting our children grow up.

We all know how to be a mother, and few of us are eager to graduate to being a crone. Still, becoming a queen is rather uncharted waters. What would it be like to claim our next stage in life? What are the hallmarks of being a queen?

Queens are sovereign. We are all queens of our own lives and our world. A queen accepts responsibility for her own decisions. She expects and deserves respect. She honors the counsel of others, but makes her own decisions. She gives advice and counsel when asked, but does not take responsibility for other people's lives. She is no longer a caretaker. Instead, she gives wise advice when it is requested and then lets go of the outcome.

Queens have struggled to get to where they are. They have earned their authority and respect and thus don't need verification of it from other people. They are, simply, The Queen.

No matter what we call ourselves, those of us of the elder generation can once again regain our former places of honor and respect in society. By fostering our intuition and acting upon the wisdom we receive in that fashion, we can once more become guides to the young. It is up to us to claim this role. It is not likely to just be handed to us. We must refuse to become invisible. It is not really about our waiting to be valued and respected. It is our responsibility to step forward and claim our power.

We are rather a large force to be reckoned with, after all. The so-called "baby boomers" (all seventy-eight million of us) are now becoming, if not elders, at least elderly. The oldest of the boomers turns age sixty-five in 2011. Interestingly enough, 2012 is the year that has been prophesied for centuries as being a time of major upheaval and change for our society. It is fascinating to ponder if there is a correlation between the prophecy and the coming of age of us as elders.

The word "elderly" has developed so many negative connotations that very few of us wish to embrace it as a self description. There is, frankly, no good word to describe those of us between the ages of fifty and eighty. Few of us desire to be called elderly at that age and we are rather kidding ourselves to think we are middle-aged. The word "senior," or worse, "senior citizen," reminds us of early-bird dining specials and low-rent highrises. Without a label, we tend to become invisible, even though our economic and political powers are as high as they have ever been.

It is, in my opinion, time for the elder generation to embrace our role as elders. We will, as we have always done, rewrite the job description. Perhaps our most important and final job on this planet is to become an elder wise person who passes on intuitive knowledge to "the seventh generation to come."

One of the things many of the respondents indicated is that they were seeing psychic ability in their children, and more often, in their grandchildren. As we embrace our own psychic ability, we also recognize it in others. As elders, we can encourage children to claim this skill. We can advise their parents to nurture rather than discount psychic ability and imagination. It is part of our function to ensure that the next generation perhaps will not need to wait until their older years to discover and embrace their psychic talents.

Joan wrote to say, "I have seven grandchildren. Six of them have seen spirits on more than one occasion. My oldest grandson has had many, many experiences with spirits, angels, and elementals. I believe he's truly gifted with a psychic ability. One example that we get a kick out of is when he looked out the bathroom window upstairs in my house where he saw an elf fly by on a golf cart (I have a golf cart), and another elf was running beside him. Another time my grandson saw an elf in my backyard by the swing set. He saw my grandson looking at him, so the elf start digging in under the swing set to disappear. I have an evergreen in the backyard where my grandson senses the elves live."

Deborah tells of how her three-year-old granddaughter saw an angel in a cloud. "We were driving to my house, she (the granddaughter) was in her car seat in the back seat. She was looking to the right out the car window and had this huge smile on her face. I asked her what she was all smiles about and she said, 'Grandma, Grandma, there's a huge angel out there.' I had to bend my head down to look out my right window and there it was, as huge as can be. A real angel in the clouds."

How lucky Joan's and Deborah's grandchildren are to have them in their lives! They are supportive of the children's visions and name them for what they are. Unlike many parents and grandparents, they don't tell their grandchildren that they are "making up stories about elves" or laugh that they have imaginary friends or are seeing things in the clouds. Rather, they are loving and encouraging and nurturing of the children's natural psychic abilities.

Some of my respondents were less certain as to how they should respond to their grandchildren's natural psychic visions. Rose asked me, "I have been watching my granddaughter grow for the past four years. I cannot believe some of the things she says and does. I sometimes question how she knows about certain things. Could she have brought them with her from another life? How can she be so intuitive at an early age? Why was she so scared when she first arrived? What lies ahead for her? Does she have a 'gift'? What does the future hold for me? What does the future hold for our country?"

These sorts of questions are what we, as elders, need to ask and hopefully answer. We have the time, the resources, and the ability to not only ponder questions like this, but also to find answers. As Rose continues to nurture her own ability, she will feel more comfortable in gently guiding her small granddaughter to accept and use her psychic ability, rather than hide or lose it as so many of us did when we were young.

Sheri told me that during what she calls her "psychic awakening," she had difficulty telling people about it. The only one who truly "got it" was her thirteen-year-old daughter. Sheri wrote, "I didn't need to tell my then thirteen-year-old daughter (about her psychic awakening). She was going through her own awakening and she knew before I told her about my being psychic, when she was finally ready to talk to me about what was going on with her."

Imagine how wonderful it must have been for Sheri's thirteen-year-old to be able to talk to her mother about what was happening to her. So few of us felt free to do that with our own mothers. Just by acknowledging and listening to our children's and grandchildren's visions and experiences, we can change the world and foster our society's transformation and evolution into a new species of intuitive beings.

Cheryl writes: "I was at the birth of my first biological grandchild at age forty-eight. It was an amazing moment. The moment I saw her the first thing that came to my mind was that I felt that I knew her and had known her for a long time. It was a feeling I couldn't shake. As she grew and started having imaginary friends, or in her case, a whole family, I knew that she had some psychic abilities. She was very sensitive to other people's moods and feelings and it seemed to cause her a lot of trouble. It was funny, but at that time I could see this in her, but I didn't see it in myself. It was about that time that her mother started reading a book by Sylvia Browne that she gave to me and we started wondering what was going on."

In Cheryl's case, the birth of her grandchild helped her to awaken to her intuition. A few years later, she still feels psychically connected to her granddaughter. She is helping both the child and the whole family to accept and acknowledge this special bond.

As we incorporate who we are into our real lives, all sorts of wonderful things happen. One of my students has worked as a schoolteacher for many years. As she awakened to her psychic ability, she subtly incorporated some of her intuitive knowledge into her work. Paula works with children with special needs, and has learned that using rocks and trees and the natural world in her teaching has aided the children in amazing ways. For example, she will have them hold a rock and then ask them what the rock is telling them.

She wrote: "I have some interesting stories about talking with nature and several trees who gave important messages, and a few flowers, stones, and boulders, too. As a teacher, my students used to say, 'She talks to trees.' I would tell them, 'It isn't anything too special to talk to trees…it's when they talk back—now that's special!'"

Yes, that is special. And so is Paula. Soon, I believe, intuitive training will be taught in our school systems. If we would only start teaching our young children to listen to their gut feelings and their inner voices, the world would be a much kinder and easier place for them to grow up in. It is teachers like Paula who are leading the way.

five
....

Illness as a Wake-Up Call

Before we can take our place as the elders, sages, shamans, and queens of society, we need to wake up and embrace our psychic ability. This awakening can take place in many ways and these ways are best described by the stories given to me by the respondents.

One of the questions asked in the survey was "Do you feel that your interest in psychic things and/or your psychic ability has changed since or around age fifty? If so, did anything trigger these abilities or change in abilities?" The responses to this question were numerous and varied.

Many of the answers, though, came from stories rather like mine. A significant and often sudden illness is a very common wake-up call to remind us of our significant connection to the world of spirit and its psychic whispers.

Maggie's story is remarkably similar to my own in many ways. While she believes she has always had psychic ability, it increased dramatically after she had a stroke at age forty. As she tells it: "At age forty, I had my first stroke. While in the ER, I suddenly found myself up in the corner of the room watching everything that the doctors and nurses were doing to me. Then I found myself in the home of a couple that I worked with. They were from Serbia and always spoke to each other in their native tongue.

"As I hovered above them, I could see that my friend and her husband were talking and she was crying. Even though they spoke in Serbian, I could understand every word they were saying. (I had never been in their home.) When I finally left the hospital and went back to work weeks later, I approached her with trepidation. I told her I had something to tell her and that she might find it hard to believe. I knew it might be hard to explain to her because of the language difference, but I knew I had to try. I told her about my experience while in the hospital. I told her that I saw her crying. I told her that I knew she had a decision to make that she was struggling with, but that it was going to be okay. I said that the move would be a very wise decision in the long run.

"She looked at me with wide eyes, then ran and got her husband and made me explain it all to him. (I thought that she hadn't understood what I was trying to say!) When I explained it all to him, he just stared at me, and I apologized for not making any sense, and both of them at the same time said nooooooo! They explained that there is *no* way I could have known what happened in their discussion that day. Even though I repeated what they had talked about, they wanted to *know* how I knew. Again, I explained as best I could. Then both proceeded to tell me something they hadn't told another soul yet. They had a job offer in Minnesota, a very lucrative one, but they both loved where they were living and were afraid to make the move. I said, 'Yes, I know, but you accepted the job offer, and you made a *very* wise choice!' They still were in shock that I knew all of this!"

This experience changed Maggie in many ways. She went on to say: "Upon leaving the hospital and for several years after, when I exited the doors…everything seemed to have a new clarity, sharper images, brighter colors, crisper sound. It was like I was seeing the world through a new set of eyes and ears."

That is a rather common (and lovely) side effect of having a psychic incident. It is as if your eyes see clearer and your mind processes information more sharply. Many people report a much more acute sense of smell, more vivid eyesight, and increased hearing ability. Sometimes it fades after a while, but often the person remains in this hyper-aware state for the rest of their life.

Most of the awakenings triggered by a physical illness are not quite as dramatic as Maggie's was. Brad Walton, a former radio personality and author, told me that he "always believed that there were people who, with varying degrees of capacity, had a gift that allowed them to see and read across time." He went on to say: "My own intuitive sensitivities and my interest and communication with those who have psychic abilities has increased since my open-heart surgery in 1999."

Brad has documented many of these intuitive happenings in his book *How Does the Heart Know Love*. He was forty-eight at the time of his surgery. He says that after this surgery he "felt an increase in my intuitive, or 'psychic,' abilities."

Gloria wrote to say that in her mid-forties she was "diagnosed with a multitude of autoimmune diseases, some of which are potentially life threatening, and which have no cure and unknown etiology." She also had spinal fusion surgery, which left her "depressed and anxious." As we so often do, Gloria did not discuss her depression and anxiety with anyone. Instead, she says, "In order to make it through that time I turned into myself and tuned in to my psychic being. It gave me the strength to work through and understand the process of healing and growth I was to experience from this."

Since that time, Gloria has noticed that "as I age, I am more in tune to the possibilities and experiences of being intuitive." She describes vivid visitations from her dead father and others. She wrote: "I sleep less and not soundly. I wake often to a sound, a vision that is there and then gone. The television turns on and then off by itself, the computer turns on and off. The most common thing is the turning on of our satellite television. It happens almost nightly. There is no sound, no picture—just the box turns on and the green or blue light showing it is on. The toilet flushes and no one is there. I always ask who is visiting. Sometimes I am scared and other times I welcome the visits. I don't understand that."

Other people report that a sudden illness brought with it a sense of introspection that increased their psychic ability. Steve, a former insurance adjuster, wrote, "I almost died from an accident in 1993 and again from an illness in 1998. The long periods of forced rest in bed allowed my mind to expand and I thought of many things to pass the time and communicated with others (past and present) while doing so. These communications became second nature and I believe became normal to me as I just accepted them."

As we age, most of our lives become more solitary. Our children leave home, we may divorce or become widowed, and we generally work less or retire. Over 75 percent of the people who answered the survey noted that one of the changes they had noticed in their lives was a desire to spend more time alone, and to spend more time in meditation and contemplation.

Steve went on to say: "I have several 'conditions' that have affected me, such as depression and anemia. The medications I take (for these conditions) have produced *vivid* dreams and less physical activity, and more intellectual thought. I have accepted these and the changes in my life and have redirected myself to really enjoy people more than I had in the past. I have 'sort of' meditated and appreciate small things I had overlooked before (a sunrise, flowers, and events). It is hard to put into words, but I am generally directed inward and have explored my mind more, especially since I stopped working."

One of the mixed blessings of illness is that it gets your attention. It often brings on, as Steve stated, a forced time of rest and solitude. There are many ways that people can respond to these changes. Those of us in the elder generation often find that these forced restrictions bring exciting and new psychic awareness.

Susan tells this story: "At age fifty-three, I had a major stroke. Fortunately, my cognitive skills and memory were untouched by the stroke. However, the stroke paralyzed my entire right side. This event completely changed my life. I had been a manager of an IT (information technology) department and worked fourteen hours a day. Then, all of a sudden, I could not do what I was used to doing. My once-full days were now empty. The only thing I had was time. So I began checking into alternative medicine. I called about receiving healing touch. It was through conversations with the practitioner that I began to realize that I had intuitive abilities."

Bodywork is an excellent method to help us discover our intuitive abilities. I am convinced that the body remembers our psychic gifts and that bodywork of all types will help us remember who we truly are. Massage, Reiki, acupuncture, acupressure, and other kinds of bodywork can help release the knowledge and memories that our bodies store in our very tissue.

Since Susan's stroke, she continues to explore her abilities. She tells of having direct contact with spirit and says, "I'm now aware of energy. There are certain stores, restaurants, and people that I avoid. I'm also able to communicate with animals."

After a significant illness, bodies may have been weakened, but intuitive ability and spiritual strength often are greatly increased. Both Steve and Susan report an increase in their satisfaction with life due largely in part to the use of their inherent, but undiscovered until illness, psychic ability.

Illness does not always come in a completely physical form, of course. Many of the people who responded to the survey told of a psychic awakening following a bout of depression or other emotional challenge.

Depression is a common occurrence, particularly at midlife. There is, on the surface of things, much to be depressed about. After all, our bodies are changing in ways that are concerning and sometimes frightening. Often our jobs have changed, our children have left, and perhaps we no longer find satisfaction in what used to bring us joy.

Depression can last for a lifetime. Alternatively, it can be used as a catalyst to discover a new and richer way to live.

Shelly tells it this way: "I experienced a multitude of physical diseases in my forties, along with a severe depression. I believe my depression and illnesses were because I did not channel my psychic abilities and allow them to flow through me. This caused energy to back up and have nowhere to go. I felt as if my body did not know what else to do except become ill. As soon as I became aware of this and began to use my abilities, the illness lifted and I felt vibrant and healthy once again. (You can ask my friends...they are still astonished at my recovery.)"

In my experience, Shelly has described it perfectly. I would estimate that at least a quarter of the people who initially come to see me are suffering from some level of depression. Psychic ability can only be squelched for so long before it has to go somewhere. For some of us, it shows itself as a form of physical illness. For others, the body just shuts down, and goes into what we call a depression.

One of my students, Peggy, described it this way: "A bout with depression (actually, I think it was severe boredom caused by not taking control of my life and making choices) made me change my life because I didn't have the energy to continue farming. This showed me that change was possible. It also created the time for me to read everything I could get my hands on about psychic ability, metaphysical information, intuition development, energy, other worlds, the unseen and triggered a strong interest in learning astrology."

After losing spouses, children, jobs, and health (among other things), depression appears, on the surface of things, to be a natural reaction. After so many emotional hits, it is commonplace to shut down physically and emotionally. Exhaustion and boredom are common symptoms of psychic ability that is not acknowledged and utilized. It seems easier, somehow, to numb our emotions and not feel anything.

Intuitive knowing has a difficult time breaking through this numbness. But, when we let it in, it acts as a sort of natural anti-depressant. Julie wrote me to say that in her fifties, "My husband was diagnosed with a brain tumor. My financial future slipped away. The company where I worked for thirty years had gone through several owners and become unstable. All of my peers were able to retire. I became depressed and took medication. I was always really scared."

Reading that list of happenings, all I could think was, "Who wouldn't be?" Julie described herself as having a "sad, sad, feeling like I was on the fringe of the rest of the world."

For a while, Julie coped as many of us do when hit with a series of disasters. As she put it, "I pretty much popped Prozac and drank wine for a while. I made my work and work friends 'my tribe.'"

Then, one day, her intuitive mind stepped in. It was a small event, but it started her on a path to clarity. Some part of Julie knew she was naturally intuitive. She told me that she had always gotten feelings about things that were always right. So, one day about two years ago, when she had an intuitive feeling, she acted upon it.

She describes it this way: "I was on the computer and began to think about a friend of mine that I hadn't heard from in four or five years. My life had become very complicated during that time and I had withdrawn from many relationships. Laurie and I had been best friends in junior high school. So, that Sunday evening I googled Laurie ... totally out of the blue. Her tiny little obituary popped up in the Brainerd (Minnesota) newspaper. She had died in California, and her memorial was to be the following Tuesday.

"Laurie had been adopted and her 'parents' never understood or really even liked Laurie. They had been estranged for several years. Laurie hadn't even listed them as next of kin so it had taken the police a few weeks to locate them. Anyway, I drove up to the memorial service. Laurie's parents' friends were there, even ones who had never known Laurie, including an aunt and cousin. I was able to speak at the service about the real Laurie that I knew."

What is remarkable about Julie's story is not the intuitive hit about the death of a childhood friend. It is that this event acted as a type of wake-up call for her. She realized, in a moment of clarity, that she *was* an intuitive and that she desired to learn more about it.

While Julie still considers herself to be alone and sad, her depression is lifting. She told me, "I decided to stop the Prozac and find a new place to belong. My intuitive thoughts are more clear now." Julie is starting to attend intuitive meetings and gatherings, and is feeling far less isolated and alone.

Addiction is often a symptom of unexpressed psychic ability. It is common to drink or use drugs as a way to "stop the messages." Of course, it doesn't work that way and usually makes things worse. Many of my respondents told tales of masking their psychic awareness with drugs and alcohol.

Ann says that she "had a relapse into active alcoholism in 2000 after fourteen years of sobriety. I was 'out' for seven years. I went to the brink and, for a reason not yet known, I survived. I lost my drivers license for four years and spent a lot of time outdoors, just getting to and from home and work. I began to see color, auras, and devic energy in my outdoor sojourns, but didn't know what to make of it. I still am in a place of not knowing what to do with all this new information, though I have spent a year doing automatic journaling and being in contact with my guides. I'm new at this, and don't have a whole lot of guidance. I am studying healing touch and have been amazed at how these new gifts help me in my service."

For several years after my own illness in 1981, I took far too many painkillers. I was in acute physical pain, but I now realize it was also a way to hide the emotional pain I was in. I had discovered that all of my goals meant nothing and that life was tenuous at best. Hiding in a fog seemed like a good option at the time.

The salvation for Ann and me, and thousands of others, was embracing our inner psychic and spiritual selves. As we did so, the need and desire for a chemical way to hide lessened. Embracing our intuitive paths, while perhaps not a cure for addiction, is certainly one step toward wholeness. One of my dreams and goals is to see intuitive development taught in the various rehabilitation centers in our world, along with other methods for attaining and maintaining sobriety.

As we age, we will experience physical and emotional difficulties. This is a fact of life. The good news about being a part of the elder generation is that there is hope and a solution.

Luckily, we have always had a few overachievers in our midst who hit their "crisis" early and have gone on to show us the way. They often tend to be people, like myself, who have early illnesses or traumas and who have used these happenings to develop their intuition and spiritual connection with the Divine.

Consider the case of Lonny Brown, whose story is detailed in his book *Enlightenment in Our Time*. I met Lonny when we were both guest speakers on a metaphysically themed cruise in 1995. Lonny was handsome, lithe, and taught yoga and healing. You would never have known that he suffered from a congenital degenerative spinal condition, complicated by several injuries, that resulted in chronic pain and episodes of partial paralysis.

This and a bout of severely debilitating rheumatoid arthritis in his early twenties made him keenly interested in self-healing and eventually led to his profession as a holistic health counselor and educator. If you were to see Lonny today at age sixty-one, you would see what appears to be a picture of perfect health. His struggles not only helped him to heal himself, but also others.

He wrote to me recently, saying, "This past summer I saved a woman's life by reaching down her throat and creating an air passage. I intuitively knew exactly what to do and had a total out-of-body experience at the same time! Believe it or not, I was so in tune with what was happening that it was actually fun. I didn't really get excited until after it was all over. Then there was plenty of thanksgiving to go around!"

Another healer and friend is Shelli Kae-Stanger Nelson. Diagnosed with diabetes at age ten, she gradually lost her eyesight and kidney and pancreas functions. Instead of allowing these horrible things to disable her, Shelli turned inward, searching for and finding her own inner strength and source of healing. She is now a gifted medium, healer, and psychic who teaches classes and aids her students in an amazing fashion. Following a pancreas and kidney transplant this year, Shelli has emerged even stronger and more vital than before. Here is what she says about the use of her intuitive ability: "What I've done to compensate for my vision loss is to hyper-expand my auric field. A person gets tons of information through the auric field. It is extremely sensitive. This expansion allows me to feel, see, hear, and know what is going on in a room, both with physical and nonphysical beings. I use my intuition as a healer to get information about my clients and to interpret what is going on in their bodies and energy field and to listen to my guides and theirs. Blindness actually makes me a better healer and channel for my clients because I'm not misled by what my eyes see."

Imagine a world in which we all used our challenges in the way Shelli and Lonny use theirs. This is one of the gifts of being part of the elder generation. We have the opportunity to take the physical, emotional, and addictive challenges that life serves to us, and turn them into something that aids not only ourselves, but others.

Sometimes, illness gives us a wake-up call and it takes us a while to realize that we received it. Here is an excerpt from an e-mail I received from Tammy, who had discovered my website through a series of synchronistic events:

"I read with interest your writing about the elder generation. At first it was just interesting…but then I realized that I did almost die in June of 2007. I had a hysterectomy that went bad in recovery. The hospital staff had to rush me back to the OR without an anesthesiologist ready (thankfully one met them there). I had developed a two-liter (think pop-bottle-size) blood clot under my liver, and I was minutes from not remaining here.

"That time was interesting. I was aware of the chaos of the crisis until I passed out from the blood clot. I remember some of the following days in the hospital and being grateful I was still here for my children (as they were very freaked out that I had almost died). I also remember being mad that I had not had an NDE (near-death experience). I didn't see angels or a white light or hang above my body during the surgery."

Tammy goes on to say, "But what I wasn't conscious of until I read through your website was that I have had a heightened sense of intuition since that time, much of which I have been ignoring. I also have a desire now to do something with it—and I really didn't before. I am wondering if my near passing did not trigger some of this. Not that I believe my story is printworthy. I just found it to be of interest to me."

Well, I believe her story is very printworthy. It illustrates an important point of all this. Often, we don't see or understand the effect things have upon us until quite a while after they have happened.

Tammy went on to describe where she is right now on her intuitive journey. "The past few years there have been instances where I have had encounters that I cannot explain. I have had deer speak to me. I have had moments where someone has asked me something and I do what I call puking...where the information comes out of nowhere and I tell them what I believe will occur...and it has been fairly accurate. I have sort of half-heartedly wanted to develop some sort of psychic/intuitive ability, but quite frankly was also afraid of suddenly hearing voices I couldn't turn off, or seeing dead people."

I smiled when I read Tammy's e-mail. "Yes, Tammy," I thought, "like it or not, you are part of the elder generation." Tammy now has a choice to make. She can continue to ignore her abilities and try to turn them off, or she can cultivate and use them to her advantage and to the benefit of the world.

It seems there are two factors in developing intuition in midlife. One is a crisis or occurrence that triggers a type of awakening. The other is taking the time (either because of depression or illness or awareness) to allow yourself to cultivate it.

Sometimes the trigger is just a feeling of nothing being quite right in your life. Joanie explains: "Nothing really happened, such as a death, or a traumatic event. I think that I just became very tired of being here, of living in the pain of the day-to-day world. I thought that there needed to be more to life than this experience. Reiki (a form of energy healing) was the first thing that became interesting to me. Then I wanted to learn more about intuition, so I sought out teachers. I have always been an artist, and I wanted to know more about the creative side, the intuitive side, and our connections with the Divine."

Dar expands on that feeling: "I had lost all hope of there being anything more than the mundane pattern of my life. That was in 2003. In the spring of 2005, I woke up, or began to wake up—I'm not sure which. Then I descended into the pits of hell and had to work my way out, learning all the way. I had help, though I can name only a few of those who have helped me and still remain with me. I am noticing a new depth inside of myself. I like it, very much."

Terese began her intuitive awakening by feeling what I sometimes call "the itch that you cannot scratch." As she puts it, "Nearing my mid-forties, I started to hear myself say frequently, 'There has to be more to life than this.' It wasn't long after I started verbally stating 'there was more to life than this' when along came my childhood friend Nina. I told her how I was feeling and she said, 'Ah, come out West.' So I did. I left a good job that I worked hard to get, stability, family, and friends on a quest to find 'more' to life in Northern California. And boy, did I. I found the magic and mystique of life. And the knowing that I have the answers within and that I am not alone on this journey called life."

Today, at age forty-eight, Terese describes herself as "on a quest to learn more of the spirit world through trainings, books, CDs, film, and friends."

Illness, depression, addiction, and death are a very real part of our human experience. The exciting thing for me is to watch and hear from those of us who have taken those experiences and used them to find our core essence of intuitive ability and spiritual knowing. As we will discover in this book, those that do are happier, more satisfied, and, like Dar, "like it, very much."

six

Death of a Child

People have often said to me, "Parents should never have to deal with the death of a child. It's against the natural order of things." Unfortunately, natural order or not, it is not uncommon for parents to lose a child. It is heartbreaking and life changing, whether the child dies young or as an adult.

The death of an adult child is sometimes made even more painful because others may not acknowledge the significance of the loss as being as severe because the lost person was an adult. Regardless of the age of the child, when you lose a son or daughter, part of your self is gone. In the case of mothers, part of your physical self is gone—the body that grew within you. For both fathers and mothers, the sense of family definition has undergone severe change. Hopes must be abandoned and expectations released. Every holiday and birthday becomes a time of painful memories and lost dreams.

The ramifications of the death of a child remain with the parents through their lifetimes. Whether through illness, accident, or any other cause, the death of a child changes the life of the parents and the siblings.

When the circumstances of the death are sudden or violent, the parents are tossed into a river of emotions without warning. At the same time, they are often required to deal with a myriad of responsibilities, demands, and painful intrusions (from the judicial system, the media, the medical world) that result from the violent death.

While still in a state of numbness, they have to make funeral plans, give statements, and attend to what seems to be an endless stream of details. After the numbness wears off, what is left is an enormous sense of grief and confusion. Sometimes, in the midst of this emotional fury, intuition emerges to lend a helping hand.

For some, after the shock comes guilt. Then, hopefully, there is acceptance. Eventually the surviving family members begin to slowly put their lives back together. At least, that is the accepted description of what happens upon the death of a child.

Sometimes, though, the death of a child, while still acutely painful, can also bring the parent to a new level of intuitive awareness. Such was the case with Kim. Kim had been interested in psychic phenomena before her daughter's death, but just as a minor interest. She also had a number of premonitions of her daughter's death, but was not aware of their significance until much later.

This is common. What is uncommon with Kim was that she took the horror that was the death of a child and used it to develop her own amazing psychic ability. By doing so, she brought comfort and peace, not only to herself, but to other members of her family and community. Here is Kim's story, in her own words, of her loss, grief, intuitive knowing, and growth:

"I have always been interested, fascinated, and intrigued by things of the spirit...near-death experiences, out-of-body adventures, ESP, psychics, spirit communication...I found them all totally fascinating. But I had no personal experience with any of them. The fact that my daughter had to die before I could have the knowingness to tap into these spiritual gifts makes me more than a little angry. Yet I know that if she had not left this world for the next, I would not be in this very holy, spiritual place that I now find myself today.

"Now, I suspect that there are many people who find these subjects to be fascinating...but it ends there—with just a fascination. It was that way for me for the first forty-nine years of my life. However, that all changed on September 20, 2003. That was the day that my oldest daughter, Elizabeth, died very tragically, very suddenly and very unexpectedly. But that was also the day that a new world opened its door for me and I walked through.

"My husband and I were on a fishing trip when we learned that our beautiful daughter and her two housemates, Amanda and Brian, had been killed in a house fire at their duplex near the University. But a very curious and amazing thing happened through the first week after her death. I learned that three people had received a "sign" from Liz, and that she was okay and not to worry. The first to tell me was Cassie, one of Liz's closest high school friends. She came through the line at the funeral home. She hugged me, and then she stepped back, grabbed my shoulders, looked me right in the eye, and said, 'Kim, I just want you to know Liz has come to me and let me know that she is okay.' A day after the funeral, my mom was back at the cemetery. As she stood and stared at the overturned earth and the flowers that were strewn upon it, she thought to herself, 'Liz, if you're okay, please give me a sign.' After a few more minutes, she turned and started to walk back home. Suddenly, seemingly out of nowhere, two monarch butterflies flew up right in front of her.

"It was perfect, because my mom was insistent that we should release butterflies at the committal service at the cemetery. It was a good idea, but no one knew where to find butterflies, not even the florist. Mom would not be deterred. She went on the Internet, found a company in California that supplied butterflies, ordered them, and had them delivered in time for the service. Quite a feat for someone who even on a good day had trouble remembering how to check her e-mail. So, two butterflies flying up in front of her made complete sense, and she understood it was a sign.

"A few days later, my husband went to the burned-out duplex to retrieve a few of Liz's belongings. He was alone in the jeep with only his thoughts and the highway to keep him company. He told me later that he was thinking about all of the events of the previous week and he thought to himself, 'Well, I'm bringing her stuff home, but I sure wish I was bringing her home instead.' Then he heard his daughter's voice, loud and crystal clear: 'I'm already home, Dad,' she said."

It didn't take long before Kim herself was receiving signs and messages from Liz. She goes on to say that a month or so after the deaths, "Our other daughter, Anna, came home from school, and Roger came home from work. We had supper, and Roger and Anna went into the computer room to download some pictures. I cleaned up the kitchen, and as I put the last of the dishes in the cupboard, our smoke alarm went off. It was blaring, and I couldn't tell which part of the house it was coming from. I ran downstairs through the family room and each of the girl's bedrooms. There was no smoke or any sign of a fire anywhere, and still the alarm continued to blare.

"I ran back upstairs through the laundry room, the kitchen, the dining room, and the living room, and down the hall to the bedrooms. I got halfway down the hall and the alarm just quit. I stopped short and stood there dumbfounded. 'Our alarms have never gone off like that before,' I thought to myself. I could hear Roger and Anna talking as if nothing had happened. Then I realized—they didn't hear the alarm. And it hit me like a ton of bricks. That was Liz! It made perfect sense! A smoke alarm on the one-month anniversary? Of course!"

Signs such as these are common after the death of a loved one. Spirits, of course, are no longer solid. Despite what you see in the media, spirits rarely materialize as beings that can physically appear, touch you, or move things. They are energy (in this dimension) and they primarily affect things that are sensitive to energy. It is common for radios to change stations or televisions to turn on and off. It is also common for other electronic devices (such as smoke detectors) to react to the presence of spirits in the room.

Once a year I lead a spiritual retreat at a lovely resort in northern Minnesota. The manager of the resort, who is a very kind man, is also very skeptical, and, I think, a little afraid of us.

Last year, on the second night of the retreat, following a powerful psychic session, the smoke alarms in the building went off four or five separate times. The staff would turn the alarm off, only to have it blare again a few hours later. Finally, the city fire inspector and fire department arrived, but could find no reason for the alarm.

I laughed when I heard that the manager believed that my group's "energy" had triggered the alarm. After all, this was coming from a so-called skeptic. I also chuckled though, to learn that the alarms went back to normal the day we all left. Be warned that one of the things you may find, when doing psychic work, is that electronic items act strangely around you. (The following year at the retreat, the staff threatened to turn off the alarms until we left.)

I received many letters and e-mails from people who had received signs of hope and love from their deceased children. Carole wrote: "After losing my twenty-three-year-old son who suffered from depression and committed suicide, I first heard from him about a month later. I was home alone, reading a book, when I heard music in the air. It was high-pitched, an array of notes, loud and clear, and lasted several seconds. I knew it was from Kenny and I thanked him for letting me know he was okay. Also, an angel figurine in our curio cabinet lit up without anyone turning the switch."

Pam, who, like Kim, lost a child in a house fire, wrote: "I have had several instances where Cody was present and made it clear that he was involved in the situation. We hold a golf tournament each year on the anniversary of his death as a scholarship fundraiser. The morning of the event in the second year, all the smoke alarms went off in our house (Cody died in a fire). They rang out for about fifteen minutes and then stopped.

"The third year, as I was preparing for the event in Cody's old bedroom (converted to an art room/office), the smoke alarm in that room chirped three times— once for each year he'd been gone."

Spirits are *not* ghosts. It may seem a little strange coming from someone like me, but I don't really believe in ghosts, at least in the way they are commonly thought of. I use the term "spirits" to describe souls of people who have died and passed on to what I call the realm of spirit. Some people refer to it as heaven or by many other terms. Whatever you call it, the soul has left the body and yet continues to have a vibrant and joyful life in another realm. They can try to communicate with us ... and they do. But they do not stay here in the earth plane, stuck and haunting us.

In the many years I have been doing this work and having talked to hundreds of spirits, I have yet to meet what others describe as a ghost. What I have seen, often, are places in which there is an energy loop that contains some of the features and memories of someone who has passed. This is, I believe, what some people mean when they see what they call ghosts.

The best way I can describe this phenomenon is that it is similar to a morphic field. The term "morphic field" was coined by Rupert Sheldrake, who, in studying plant mutations, learned that cell patterns have a type of memory, not explainable only by genetics. This memory, which Sheldrake called "morphic resonance," increases the likelihood that mutations will recur. The memory extends beyond the cells and into magnetic fields far beyond the surface of the earth.

Strong emotions, such as those that happen in violent deaths, also create a type of morphic field. It is an energy "loop" that replays over and over again in the same location. In a "haunted" location, I often see these energy or memory loops. The emotions, often of fear and sadness, are very real. Sometimes there is even a type of wispy image that can be seen, or a sort of cold emptiness.

This is very real. What it is not, though, is a spirit caught between the realms and longing to go to the light. It is nothing to be afraid of, and the pattern can be rather easily dispersed though positive intention and clearing of the energy field.

Our loved ones who have passed very much wish to communicate with us to give us comfort and to let us know they are okay. They can do that in a number of ways. These are not ghostly hauntings; they are gifts from those who love us.

It is not uncommon for the spirits of our children to visit us to let us know that they are okay. Joan's daughter came to her with a message of hope. Joan told me: "I lost my sixteen-year-old daughter, Christina, in a car crash on May 30, 1987. It was such a shock for this to have happened. Her birthday was on August 22, and as the day neared, something kept building inside of me. When the day came, I was missing my daughter so much and what was building inside of me came to a head by bedtime. I remember crying uncontrollably. After I regained control of myself, I decided to go upstairs and sleep in her bed because I needed to be near what was hers. I dozed off after a while, only to wake up again and stare at the ceiling. This went on until around three a.m. As I was staring into the darkness, I saw a seven-foot-tall angel appear at the left side of the foot end of the bed. Then my daughter appeared, but only her head. It was encircled in a halo of colored light. Christina disappeared as quickly as she had come. Then I sensed the angel come to the side of the bed. At that point, I went quickly down the stairs to my own bed."

After that happened, Joan went on to say, "I became more aware of another realm after losing my daughter. My faith in God changed. I still believe in him very strongly, but in a different way."

Sometimes we can feel the actual physical presence of a spirit by a touch or an indentation on the bed or sofa. Often we can feel an energy shift in a room or house. It is as if the very air has changed in some fashion. The energy vibration of a spirit can make itself known in that way as a very real physical presence.

After the death of her adult daughter in 2003, Kathleen said, "For five months after my daughter's death, I felt euphoria when I opened the door to come into the house. The door opened to the exact spot where I found her dead. I believe that she softened the blow of the shock by creating an environment of joy. It can only be described as such. I cried for two years back and forth to work, yet when I opened the door there was this fabulous joy in the house."

Spirits can sometimes request animals, birds, and insects to act in a way that gives their loved ones a sign. It is very common for birds to appear in an unusual fashion following the death of a loved one. Kim's story about the butterflies is also one I have heard (in variations) many times before. We know that animals can see and hear things out of our range of vision and hearing. Carole and many others have told me that their cats often stare at something in the room that no one else sees. In Carole's case, she believes that it is her deceased son Kenny's spirit that is attracting the cat's attention.

Spirits do seem to be able to influence some part of the material world, although they tell me this is much more difficult to do. There are many tales though, of pennies being left in unusual places, things being moved or indentations being left by an unseen body. Pam told me that "pennies show up all the time. Once there was a trail up our garage steps all the way to the back door."

Here is one of the most amazing stories I received about signs from a departed child. Cindy wrote: "My story begins like this. My stepson, whom I'd helped raise since he was eight, was killed in an automobile accident on Sept. 21, 2007. August 9, 2008, would have been his thirtieth birthday. In his honor our family rented Harleys that day and took a road trip to let Bryan know how much we missed him. We wanted to do something he would have loved to have done.

"My son loved his Harley and had a passion to ride. I myself hadn't been on a motorcycle in over twenty-five years. My husband continues to ride when he can find a bike, and on this special trip I actually went along on this memorial ride. Bryan would have been so excited for me; he always said I would love it. Anyway, the entire day was just beautiful, and we found that memories of our son filled our hearts.

"After riding a couple of hours from home we all decided to stop for lunch in a small town somewhere we had never been and have lunch. As everyone was getting up to leave, I stayed behind to make sure we all had everything and just to enjoy the moment. Everyone went out the same way we came in to the restaurant, except when

I went out, something told me to go another way…up a small ramp to the parking lot. I did, and then something caught my eye.

"There was something green stuffed into a small crack in the concrete by the wall. I looked at the object and saw the initials BW (my son's), which was so strange that I looked closer. Then I saw the name White, my son's last name. 'Okay,' I thought, 'this is just too bizarre!' I turned the object with my foot, and there it was, his entire name spelled out…Bryan White!

"All I could do was scream for my husband and oldest son to come look at something I thought I had seen. I covered the object with my foot until they arrived. I don't know if I did that because I was unsure of what I found or afraid it would go away. When my husband arrived, he pulled it out of the crack. It was a rubber can holder (something my son used all the time) with his initials and full name under it."

Cindy goes on to add: "This is my story of hope and comfort to all of us who have lost someone we love. We have to believe in the fact that they continue to touch our lives and want us to know they are there by our side. There is no other explanation for me as to why I found that item in a small town that I couldn't even tell you the name of, except I was meant to find it and to believe Bryan placed it there."

Most of the signs given to us by spirits are far less dramatic than Cindy's. That does not, though, suggest that they are less meaningful. After her son's death in a freak accident, Claudia fell into a deep depression.

Then, on a rainy Seattle day, on a very wet sidewalk, a soft white feather appeared, untouched by the rain. This small sign from her son was enough to help her in her grief. She wrote to say: "Just the knowledge that my son is at peace and knowing that he exists has brought me peace. I have strong visions of the way he looks and greets me. He radiates love."

What makes the survivors in this chapter unique is that they paid attention to these happenings. It is easy to say that these signs are coincidence or that they are making something out of nothing (although, in some of these cases, that would be a very *big* coincidence indeed). Even if that were true, however, it brought them comfort and purpose. They took their grief and their signs and used them as an impetus to change their lives.

Many of my respondents decided to develop their intuition and psychic gifts after receiving signs and visitations from spirits.

Kim, whose daughter died in the house fire, first started by coming to see me for a mediumship reading, but then later decided to take some of my classes in developing intuition. In her words: "I had started my journey to mastering my own intuition. I was hungry to learn more, and I decided to take some of Kathryn's intuition classes. I had no idea what to expect, but I knew it would be fun. I had a few ideas of what I wanted to learn, but I had no clue if they were at all possible. To be able to communicate with Liz (her deceased daughter) on my own was my highest priority."

Despite lack of support from her family and her fear of looking crazy (perhaps the most common reason people do not foster their intuitive skills), Kim learned and practiced her intuition. She was brave enough to write her story, which is published in the book *True Stories of Messages from Beyond*. Today, Kim tells her story to groups of people who have lost children and campaigns for fire prevention. She has become a proud member of the elder generation.

Others who responded to my questionnaire tell amazing stories of turning their grief into a positive thing that touches not only their lives but those of others. One of my favorites comes from Denise, whose son, Joe, died in May 2008.

She writes: "These days have been very hard. Today I was driving to Circuit City to get a camera. I just felt this overwhelming anxiousness. I wanted to go to the police station and sit until they talked to me. I wanted to go to the morgue and sit with my son, no matter what anyone had to say about it. I just couldn't get those thoughts out of my head.

"Then this idea came to me that I should visit the vintage guitar store where I had dropped off and picked up Joe on many occasions. I pass that area every day to and from work, but have never had the *need* to stop. Today I had to go, which was a better choice than the original thoughts for a destination.

"I had never been in that store, so I entered without any preconceived notions as to what I would find inside. As I entered I saw a young woman playing a guitar with an older gentleman. In front of them was an even older gentleman playing a keyboard. The music was an incredible mix of jazz and the blues. The three musicians were as good as any I have paid to listen to, yet there they were nestled amongst the hanging guitars and amps for sale.

"The feeling that this place was more than a store was evident and consuming. While I stood mesmerized by the performance, this nice man pulled up a stool and started telling me about his love of music and this store. I sat on the floor next to him and listened to his tale as we were serenaded by the talented regulars.

"I could see why Joe loved this place. I felt that Joe sat with me on that floor and surrounded me with assurance that I had found the right place and the right people. I had gotten a little bit of money from an addendum on my life insurance policy that included my children. Since receiving it, I wanted to spend a portion of the money on someone who loved music and needed some help affording a guitar. I was never sure how I would find this person, but I knew that Joe would lead me when it was time and where I needed to go. He did, and his timing was impeccable.

"When the man, Carl, finished his story, I told him about Joe. He remembered him but intuitively did not ask any details. He let me share what I wanted in the way and amount I wanted to. I told him that I had a little money and that I would like to give it to a struggling artist. It took him seconds to tell me that the girl playing the guitar was such a person. She had been working two jobs, one as an instructor at this shop, so that she could afford the guitar she was now playing. He told me of her kind heart and great love of music. I knew from the moment I entered the shop that she was the one, so this was just confirmation.

"When our talk was over, Carl introduced me to Liz. She is a beautiful girl. She is a senior in high school and has her heart set on a musical journey. The guitar is the one that fits her; it is a part of her. Joe would understand that. I told her about Joe, about his love of music. I told her of his death and my desire to share him with someone else who was a kindred spirit. I asked her if she would be willing to accept a gift from me in memory of my son. With teary eyes she told me that she would be honored. She told me that once she got this guitar it would be with her forever and that she would tell everyone that Joe helped her get it. She also asked me if I was a Christian. That inquiry came from nowhere, yet such a welcome question. She loved music and God, a combination I could not have even hoped for.

"We exchanged phone numbers and agreed to meet at the shop next Saturday. I will give her the money, a copy of Joe's music, a picture of him, and a video that I will make just for her. Liz will be the person whom Joe touched after his death. She will be the one who will tell the story of my beautiful son to others who would have never known of him otherwise. Today I experienced grace, love, and hope. It's all good!"

Denise was able to take the tragic death of her son and turn it into a gift to the world. She followed her intuitive knowings and the quiet urgings of Joe's spirit to the music store. And she and Liz and the world are better for it.

Carol's twenty-year-old son, Mikey, was killed in an accident in the Colorado Rockies on September 22, 2007. Carol wrote: "We found out the following morning. The news was so devastating and my heart ached in pain! I wondered how I would ever survive without my precious son. We had a fabulous relationship and we were very close. A friend of mine who had lost his wife seven years earlier told me to pay attention. He said Mikey would send us signs to let us know he was okay. He also told me to journal them as I may forget as time goes on. Well, now that I am almost done with my second notebook, I understand what he meant. My son has saved me and continues to help me through my grief.

"The signs started immediately. Our flag would blow heavily in the wind, yet there was no wind. Songs would play as though he was talking to me. You see, Mikey was a DJ while he was going to school in Fort Collins, Colorado. He was very big into what songs said. Also, for years we would play John Denver as we drove to Colorado as a family for our skiing and snowboarding trips. After he died, there were so many interesting signs with music.

"We have lights going on and off by themselves when we talk about him or to him. (I often talk out loud to Mikey, as I know he hears me.) I have had amazing dreams. He has talked to me and hugged me. I could feel him!"

Carol goes on to say, "It has not just been me who has received signs, but other family and friends as well. I have physical signs or objects that are unexplainable, and I have saved everything. At one point, we had a family friend who was dying of cancer. He told me he had seen the other side—Heaven—and it was magnificent. He told me that when he passed over and saw Mikey, he would call me. And he did! The number is locked in my phone and is a number that does not exist."

What is the most striking in Carol's story is the hope and transformation that it gave to her. She has told her story on radio and is writing it for a magazine article. As she puts it: "It is so real to me. I am a regular mom who has experienced a terrible tragedy and now continue to have amazing things happen to me. The strength and hope this gives me is amazing. I thank God for allowing this to happen. I wish other people could believe. Some think I am crazy. It is interesting to me that people believe in eternal life, yet they don't think it is possible that our loved ones can communicate with us or that they are close. It is so helpful in working through your grief. It would help so many others if only they could open their minds a little."

These stories touchingly illustrate several characteristics of members of the elder generation. They take a horrific and tragic experience and turn it into something positive, whether it is becoming intuitive, writing about it, giving a gift, speaking, or in innumerable other ways. They not only became aware of their ability to be intuitive and to talk to spirits, but they also have taken concrete steps to learn to use their intuition and gifts in a way that benefits both themselves and the world at large.

When parents can feel, in some way, a sense of their children, it relieves, at least in part, the agony of losing a child. Rather than living in a mental state where they relive the agonizing details of the death, they can talk or see or receive signs of a happy, radiant spirit who has moved beyond the circumstances of the death. They focus on remembering the positive times and the blessings of their child, rather than the tragedy of the death.

Without this comfort, many parents of children who have died become angry, lonely, and bitter. They become set apart from the rest of the world and their surroundings, and circumstances seem fragmented and unreal. Environments that once seemed safe feel threatening. The world becomes a dangerous place. The guilt is enormous as the parent goes over and over the circumstances of the death and what they could have or should have done to prevent the death.

Regardless of what we would like to believe, the world is unpredictable and chaotic. There is no direct line of cause and effect that leads from us to our loved one's death. While we may (and undoubtedly do) get premonitions of death and danger, we are usually not able to act on these premonitions in a way that would affect the outcome. Even though assuming responsibility for such a tragedy would give order to that which is disorderly and excruciatingly painful—surviving a child's death—it does not help or relieve the grief. Anything can happen at any time to anyone. No matter how loving or wise or careful we are, we cannot change the unexpected nature of death. No matter what we may see for the future, we cannot necessarily affect the outcome.

We can, however, change the nature of how we deal with death. Intuitive knowing and communicating with the child's spirit can dramatically help people come to terms with the death of a child. It does not mean they forget the circumstances of the death or that there is no longer any sadness and pain. However, it often happens that the child gradually occupies a different place in their minds and hearts, and they can adjust to life without the child's physical presence. They *know* at a deep level that while the child's body no longer exists, the child's soul is timeless. They also know that they can still communicate at some level with their child. They learn to live with the pain, not in the pain. With that knowing, the parent can learn to continue with life: to laugh, to think about other things, and to make plans for a different future. Often, that future includes a life of intuitive knowing and wisdom.

seven

....

Death of a Spouse

When a person loses their spouse, they not only lose a loved one, their whole life changes. Often there are huge financial and legal issues that have to be dealt with immediately. When the death comes suddenly, the surviving spouse's entire world is turned upside down overnight. When the death is lingering, the survivor must watch, bit by bit, as a lover, friend, companion, and lifestyle slip away. Either way, it is one of the most traumatic things in life. If we are married, at least half of us will experience this loss.

One of my areas of expertise as an attorney was probate law. The paperwork and court appearances were relatively easy compared to the counseling of the surviving spouse. Often they were in shock and unable to make decisions. Other times it seemed that they were impulsive, wanting to get it over with, as though that would somehow make the nightmare go away. As an attorney, all I could do was to be kind and try to keep the legal system from inflicting additional pain on an already fragile person.

As a medium, though, I found I could not only protect the person from further pain, I could help lessen the pain. I found that knowing that death does not end a relationship, but rather just changes it, was the key to surviving and thriving after the death of a spouse.

By this I do not mean, of course, that the survivor should deny that his or her spouse is dead. Admitting that they will never see each other again in this lifetime is a key component to healing. However, as a medium, I could show the surviving spouse that this lifetime is not forever, and that the couple would, indeed, meet again.

Studies have shown that over half of all widows have reported communication and signs from their departed spouse. One of the reasons many survivors come to see me is because they are being contacted by their deceased spouse. They are often confused, anxious, and afraid about this. Unable to talk about these happenings with their family and friends, they are terrified of being ridiculed or patronized.

Dee came to see me after her husband had died of cancer. Because he needed constant care, she had retired early in order to aid him in his last days. His death left her without love and companionship, and also without a job. Her days, which had been so full of caretaking, now seemed empty. It is little wonder that she became depressed.

When she came for her visit, she told me, "I can feel my husband's presence, and even hear his voice when I talk to him. It became apparent early on that he is still in my life, to help me deal with my missing him."

I was able to contact her husband, and, as she states: "I know it is real, because the spirits have said things through Kathryn that only that person and I would know. I would like to develop this skill more, as I have many questions and I am sure there are great conversations to be enjoyed."

After Dee first made contact with her husband, he continued to give her small signs to show her he loved her and was still with her. When alive, her husband loved to play jokes and make her laugh. It is not surprising that he continued to do so after he passed.

Dee writes: "The stories that are the most fun are the ones with my deceased husband moving items in the house. He has taken and hidden my glasses twice, he drops coins in the most interesting spots, and he continues to do fun things, like making talking toys talk. I have a Bob the Builder doll. After my husband's death the doll (without being touched) would spontaneously say 'Good Job' or 'This is going to be loud!' when I was doing a 'man type' job around our home. At one point, I said to myself, 'I haven't heard Bob the Builder for a while,' and away it would go. What fun."

She added: "I couldn't find the pendulum Kathryn had given me, so I wrote her. When she asked my husband about it, he looked at her like a kid who had been caught with his hand in the cookie jar. The pendulum appeared in the middle of my rug later that day!"

Contacting her husband that first day we met gave Dee more than hope that he was still alive "somewhere" and that she could still have contact with him. It also gave her an interest and something to become excited about.

She went on to take classes to increase her intuitive skills and now practices daily to make that a part of her life. She is one of the most joyful women I know.

Here is how she describes her life now: "In times of quiet meditation, I can feel the presence of loving and helpful spirits. My nephew died in March, leaving me devastated that I had no inkling of his depression and alcoholism. But, I have been able to talk to him. He is such a great young man, I miss him, but know he is okay.

"I am now able to find peace in the most troubling of times. I know that everything happens for a reason, and I am confident that I can hear what to do, and do it without worrying too much about it. If I ask a question prior to meditation or sleeping, I soon get the answer, and I know it is right."

Linda lost her husband when she was still quite young. She writes: "I was about thirty-seven when my husband died. We had been married seventeen years. It was a rough marriage. We had three kids. He was an alcoholic, smoker, diabetic, and had cirrhosis of the liver. I was a very religious person who taught Sunday School, went to church, and saw to it our children went. When Joe died, I prayed endlessly for God to forgive him for his sometimes mean ways and to please remember his heart was good, that it was the illness.

"About eight months after he died, I was sleeping when I dreamed that a little boy (now I believe he was my spirit guide) took me to heaven to see Joe. I remember leaving my body with this boy and seeing Joe. He was so healthy looking! He didn't say anything. He didn't have to. I asked to stay and I remember the voice, I could hear this voice with every cell of my body, even though I was not in human form, tell me it was not my time yet. I remember the place being huge. And Joe just glowed! I was brought back to my body with what seemed like a thud. It was a very loud and heavy feeling. I knew Joe was at peace after that visit, and although I still knew nothing of the paranormal world, I thanked God for showing me Joe was okay."

Dreams are one of the ways that spirits can most easily communicate with us. During the day we are so busy and our minds are so full, that we often miss communications from the other side. There are some important steps to getting intuitive information and spirit communications while dreaming. Remember how Dee said that she asks a question before meditating or sleeping? This is crucial if you want to receive intuitive information in a dream. If you want to hear from a deceased spouse, ask to see or hear him or her.

Spirits are polite; they usually wait to be asked before speaking or appearing.

Everyone dreams nightly. If we did not dream, we would become psychotic within a very short period of time. Most of us do not remember dreams because we wake up to a jarring alarm and instinctively move our body. If you set the intention before you go to sleep to speak to a spirit or to have a psychic dream, then make sure you wake slowly and without moving. Upon awakening, tell yourself your dream before getting out of bed. In this way you will remember your dreams and your spirit visits. Like all intuitive work, the more you practice dream work the better you will be at it. When you are skilled at remembering and controlling your dreams, they will bring great meaning to your life.

After Linda's night-time visit with Joe (and by the way, I completely believe that she saw him and that it was *not* just a dream), her life continued, just more peacefully. It was not until she was around fifty years of age that her next paranormal experience occurred.

As she describes it: "My daughter's house is haunted, and I am not alone on this! At first I used to laugh at my daughters when they told me about Kelly's house. I would say 'It's an old house' or 'Oh, you're just imagining things.' Then I had my first experience. It was about five a.m. I was on my way to pick up my then-infant grandson to babysit. My daughter was to be off to work, my son-in-law sleeping. As I approached their house I got the strongest feeling that my daughter was still home. The feeling was so very strong. I pulled in the driveway, still feeling as if she were there, but the outside light was on, telling me she had left. I went in expecting to see her jacket, but it was gone. Still thinking 'she's here, why didn't she tell me she was staying home?' I peeked in the bedroom; my son-in-law was asleep. All the while this incredible feeling of Kelly being there was still with me. I went to the baby's room and bent over the crib to pick him up when I saw someone going into the bathroom. I then went into the bathroom, saying 'Kelly' when all of a sudden the bathroom felt cold and empty! Kelly wasn't there and that strong feeling of her being there was gone. Nothing now but cold and empty. Needless to say, I grabbed the baby and ran. This began what I call my 'three-and-a-half-year window' into the paranormal world."

While I don't believe Linda saw a ghost (see chapter 6 on my ideas about ghosts), I do believe this experience opened Linda up to her intuitive abilities. She told of many paranormal experiences after that first event, some rather frightening, some very comforting. She began to keep a journal of her experiences, trying to make sense out of things that don't make sense. She described toys going off by themselves (rather like Dee's Bob the Builder story), as well as out-of-body experiences and other ghostly appearances.

They no longer frighten her. As she states: "I have a respect for death. Death is life. I believe that we are in death as we are in life. I want people not to be afraid of death, because that is when we truly live."

After Rose's husband died, he continued to try to reach out to her. Like many spirits, he found it easiest to show her he was present by affecting electrical and mechanical things. She wrote: "My husband passed away on January 1, 2006. He died of a heart attack in our house. On Easter, in April 2006, several lights were on in the morning when I got up. (I had turned them all off before going to bed.) I believe my husband turned on those lights to remind me that he was still with me. In April, at daylight savings change, I turned the clocks ahead one hour, except for his alarm clock. Before I went to bed, I noticed his alarm clock read 4:44 (my favorite number is four). I did not touch his clock, but when I woke up in the morning, the clock was set to the correct time."

Small occurrences such as these are repeatedly mentioned in the responses to my questionnaire. Spirits try very hard to get our attention. Rose went on to say: "I have felt a very strong presence of my husband in the house. I am not afraid of these encounters. I feel they are natural and embrace them as a token of love."

People often ask me how they can know that it is a communication from a deceased loved one, rather than merely a coincidence. One clue is that the sign you are given is often something that is only meaningful to *you*. Marie called to give me a wonderful example of this. She told me that she and a friend of hers (Dotty) have been going out to lunch after church for many years. They always go to the same restaurant and talk, laugh, and visit about their lives and other interests.

Dotty's husband had passed away only three months before their most recent meeting, and Dotty was, of course, still grieving. They had already ordered their meals, but the waitress returned to them, laying two large napkins in front of them and saying, "I thought you might need these."

As they had been given napkins previously, Marie told me that she chuckled and said to Dotty, "Do we look messy?" Then Marie noticed that Dotty's expression had changed to one of wonder. Dotty responded, "Every time my husband and I went out to eat, he always ordered two extra napkins. It used to embarrass me."

Dotty was convinced, and so am I, that the napkins were a sign from her deceased husband. Marie and Dotty asked the waitress why she had brought the extra two napkins. She puzzled a bit and admitted she really didn't know why and that it was unusual behavior for her. She just had felt a strong need to do so.

Spirits will often use other people, animals, birds, and even inanimate objects to send messages to their loved ones. Our job is to be aware when we get these messages and to trust what they are.

As if in verification, only fifteen minutes after Marie had called me with this story, she called again. She had just gotten off the phone with Dotty, she told me. Dotty had laughed when she heard that Marie had given me the napkin story. She joyfully told Marie that just that morning she had been moving some papers and other things from her dining room table, when, lo and behold, what did she discover but two napkins, ones she had never before seen in her house.

Sometimes, the surviving spouse has even less dramatic proof that they are still watched over, cared for, and loved. Shawn's beloved husband Emery died after a long battle with cancer. He had been her soul mate and best friend, and she missed him desperately. Like many people in long-term marriages, she had relied on him for many things. One of those things in their marriage was that Emery had always been the driver in the family. Shawn wrote: "Shortly after my husband Em (Emery) died, I realized I was now stuck within a truly limited driving route because, while I was a confident and capable driver for most purposes, including feeling comfortable on freeways, I had developed an unreasonable and apparently unmanageable fear of merging onto the freeways.

"Em was a great teacher. His teaching aptitude and patience had been of enormous advantage to our children as they benefited from his apparently bottomless cache of skills. He had, as a matter of fact, taught me to drive after we first met, when I was nineteen years old. However, along with his exceptional teaching skills, because of his innate kindness, Em was also the proverbial enabler. In my case, his willingness to step in and help out whenever there was a need had allowed me to avoid merging to the point of phobia, as he cheerfully drove me to any destination that required a freeway merge.

"After his death, determined not to be restricted by this phobia, I hesitantly called a local driving school, explained my problem, and was told 'we know just who can help.' I was wisely assigned to a young man every bit as patient as Em, but who also knew how to build in me enough confidence to overcome my fear. After having me drive hither and yon for a little while, he proclaimed that I was a very good driver who instinctively did just what was needed for successful merging. Shortly thereafter, on that day, I was merging onto I-494 in rush hour traffic, and the driving teacher declared I needed no more lessons.

"After my one day of lessons, it was up to me to maintain the proficiency I'd just acquired, but I was only able to force myself to continue merging by talking with Em, often out loud, beseeching him to hang in and keep me safe as I perfected this skill. He did his part; I did my part. And now I merge with the best of them, with nary a shudder. But, Em is always with me in the car (I have no doubt about this) and I still chat with him, continually telling me how proud he is of me!"

I love this story for its very simplicity. Often what we feel the most from our deceased loved one is a sense of presence and support. Many women would have let the death of a longtime spouse cripple them. Shawn did not. She faced her fear, and, with the help of Em, learned to merge. She also took her first international trip that year, heading off on a marvelous adventure to Peru with a group of spiritual wanderers. Today, five years later, she has made new friends, embarked on many adventures, and is a published writer. Oh yes, Shawn. I assure you that Em is *very* proud of you.

Whether the deceased spouse speaks in dreams, through signs, visitations, or just a sense of presence, there is one universal result: the survivor feels more joyous, more secure, and happier than before. They have been given a small glimpse into the world of spirit and their lives have been changed for the better. As we will see, often this change is dramatic and life enhancing.

eight

The Passing of Parents, Siblings, and Others in Our Lives

Of course, it is not only the death of a spouse or child that can usher in psychic awareness. Death has an interesting way of focusing our attention. When we are numb, grieving, and even in shock, we are often more open to the spirit realm and to psychic knowings than when in our usual busy state. Sometimes, as we have demonstrated in previous chapters, we are prepared for a sudden death by a series of dreams or other precognitive happenings. Terri wrote to me with an amazing story involving her brother's death. Because it is so moving, I have quoted it in its entirety.

When she was forty-eight years old, Terri's brother Tony died suddenly of a massive heart attack. She wrote: "I had two vivid dreams on two successive nights preceding the death of my brother. I was living in St. Paul, Minnesota; he and the rest of my family lived on the West Coast. I had no knowledge of Tony having heart or other physical problems, and these dreams seemed to come out of the blue.

"The first night I dreamed of being in the house where my two brothers and I grew up. Although she was out of context, my brother's only child, a daughter, 'B', was there, and we were planning to go somewhere together. I explained that I'd forgotten to pack appropriate clothing for such an event, and she told me to go look on my parents' bed where she had laid out some clothing. I went into the bedroom and there on my parents' bed (where, as children, my brothers and I would sometimes play) were two black tops made of chain mail. I remember thinking, 'Why do B and I need protection?' Then I awoke, feeling very disturbed.

"On the second night I dreamed of being attacked by a black panther. The panther attacked from behind and bit into my arm and shoulder, causing great pain. I remember calling out for my brother. I awoke and noted the time, then resumed my sleep. (Later, I learned that the hour coincided with the hour of my brother's death, which probably involved pain in his arm and shoulder.) In the morning I awoke and felt very uneasy. I couldn't explain the malaise I felt, but felt ill enough so that I decided not to go to work. I hadn't lived in

St. Paul for long, but I dressed and started walking through the residential area around my apartment. I walked and walked for hours, until I was lost. I kept looking up at the sky and thinking that the sky didn't *look* right. I could not explain the feelings I was having and feared for my sanity. I finally returned to my apartment later in the afternoon and phoned a good friend to discuss what was happening to me. She listened patiently and assured me that I probably had a little bug. We concluded our conversation and I hung up the phone. It rang immediately, and I answered to find my father's distraught voice telling me that he had just found my brother's body in his home, and that he had died of a massive heart attack around midnight the night before.

"Through my convulsive tears I called my friend back and asked her to come help me book a flight to California and get packed. While I waited, I was inconsolable and paced the small living room of the apartment where I lived. Suddenly, I was aware of a very loud buzzing sound that grew and grew until my body became almost paralyzed. I sat down, unable to continue moving. The sound enveloped me like a caress. A surge of warm energy started pulsing through my body, head to toe, or maybe it was toe to head—I can't recall. Almost instantly, I was calmed, and I knew everything would be all right. I felt that my brother was with me, helping me cope, letting me know that he was okay.

"I flew out to California and somehow had the strength to do what needed to be done, even speaking at the funeral, despite my intense fear of public speaking."

Terri goes on to say, "Actually, prior to Tony's death, my dear friend and cousin, Don, died of AIDS, then my mother died within the year (about the time of the demise of a thirteen-year romantic relationship), so I was very depressed, experiencing anxiety attacks and rarely sleeping. All of these things—although Tony's death was the real trigger—seemed to activate psychic events and vivid dreams that would no longer allow me to ignore the reality of personal psychic events. In the past, I had always made excuses for the phenomena, thinking that coincidence was the norm. I have always respected the experiences and truths of others, but until this time I had not allowed myself to acknowledge a personal relationship with paranormal experience. Fear seems to be the major factor holding us back in recognizing the paranormal."

Like so many people in this book, it took a traumatic event (in this case, her brother's death) to open a door in Terri's soul. Terri wisely admits this door was closed due to her fear. Fear…of what people will think, of being crazy, of the unknown…all of these fears keep us from acknowledging our psychic ability. Once that door is opened, however, it is difficult to securely close it again. Luckily, most of the people who have had the experience have no desire to do so, despite the consequences.

Like Terri, I lost my older sister, Ruthie, to a sudden and massive heart attack at age forty-eight. Ruthie and I had a complicated relationship, but we also had a very strong psychic connection. Ever since we were children we were able to communicate nonverbally. One game we would play when we were young was "guess a card." She would take a deck of cards and then pull one card and look at it. My job was to guess which card it was. Then we would switch, and it would be her turn to guess the card. We got to the point where we could go through the entire deck without a mistake. At that point, we became bored with the game and went on to other things. Strangely, at the time, neither of us considered what we could do anything more than a simple game and not the least bit remarkable.

As we both aged, though, a certain amount of distance and life issues decreased our closeness, although certainly not our love for each other. Ruthie seemed to always have a way of making my life complicated. Her death was no exception. I learned of her death when the police knocked on my door in the middle of the night. (For whatever reason, my telephone had decided *not* to ring that night and my panicked family had finally asked the police to go to my home.) I was grief stricken, beside myself, and most of all, furious with her. Once again, I thought, she had messed up my life.

Her memorial service was scheduled for a few days later, and I was committed to leave on a three-week European cruise as a guest lecturer. I had signed a contract and had no good way to get out of it. I felt it was important to my career and, of course, I wanted to go. And, I was really angry at her for dying at such an inconvenient time.

So, I went on the cruise. It was a transatlantic voyage and took five full days to cross from Spain to the Caribbean. During that time, with no companions and very little to do, I spent my days staring at the ocean, watching the waves, and wondering if I had done the right thing. Had I, I pondered, allowed old feelings of resentment to influence me to skip her memorial service? Or, had I done the right thing by taking care of myself? Was I truly as self-centered as I was feeling at that moment?

Although we were hundreds of miles from any land mass, a tiny bird flew out of nowhere and landed on the deck of the cruise ship. The crew was stunned and took it on as a pet, feeding it and trying to keep the poor lost thing alive. They had never seen a bird that far out to sea before. It huddled, shivering and scared, for three days on deck. Then, one day, without reason, it flew off. We docked shortly thereafter. The bird had somehow known that we were close enough to land that it would again be safe.

Somehow, the tiny lost bird became a symbol for me. I believe that Ruthie sent the bird to show me that she was not lost anymore and that, when the time was right, she too had flown back to a sheltering shore. That awareness allowed me to know that I was okay too, and, while probably still very self-centered, I had done the best I could.

Messages from spirits are like that. They need interpretation and it is up to us to decipher them according to our beliefs and life experiences. Of course, the bird landing on the ship could certainly have been a coincidence. Perhaps it was, although I will never believe it. In the end though, it doesn't matter. What matters is the message I received from my soul that allowed me to forgive myself and my sister and go on living in the best way I could.

Rene wrote to tell of his devastating loss. His twin brother died at the young age of twenty-four. In his own words, he describes what happened:

"My twin passed away when we were twenty-four years old. A few days after we buried my sweet brother, I saw him in the flesh. He didn't say anything but he just stood behind the recliner, staring at me. I think this was his way of letting me know that he is still and always will be with me. Also, about two years ago, my oldest and last living brother passed away from cancer. The day we buried him, I was going to take a nap, and I heard his voice clear as day. This is the weird part, I know it sounds crazy, but he came into my body and he wanted me to take him to the light, if you will, and I helped him get there."

Now, at age forty-seven, Rene feels these experiences have changed him. He has recently developed a strong interest in psychic experiences, taken classes, and is attempting to harness his ability to speak to spirits. Because he was awakened early to the knowledge of the spirit realm, Rene became willing to learn and study and grow in his development of his skills.

Larry also tells of an increase in awareness of intuitive abilities following the death of his father in July of 2007. Since that time, he reports, he has had "an increase in the frequency of intuitive moments. For example, I know the phone will ring shortly before it happens, and a sense of who is calling before I answer the phone. I will think of going out for dinner and later my wife will suggest it, or someone will say something in conversation just after I had the same thoughts."

As Larry allowed these intuitive moments to happen to him and began to cultivate them, an interesting thing happened. It was then that he had a direct sense of his deceased father.

He goes on to say: "I recently felt my father within me, seeing through my eyes when in a fishing boat moving across the water. As I observed the beautiful surroundings, the trees on the shoreline, that water, the early morning mist, the birds, the clouds in the sky, I was very joyfully and tearfully moved as he and I 'talked' about the beauty of the scenery. I sensed he was observing this physical world through me and enjoying it a great deal. For perhaps thirty years or more, he took me and my brothers to a northern Minnesota resort every Memorial Day weekend, and we spent many hours on the lakes, going from one to another, in search of the elusive fishing hole. We were always awed by the natural beauty of our surroundings."

Both Larry and Rene had the interesting experience of feeling a deceased loved one "inside of them" who is seeing through their eyes. This is not uncommon, as spirits often use our physical eyes to see the world. I had a similar experience myself a few years ago. I was at a book signing in Holland, in the tiny town of Wynterswyk, where my father had been born over ninety years before. I have many cousins and other relatives left there (my father emigrated to the United States in 1920) and several of them were at the book signing.

As I addressed the crowd, I suddenly felt an overwhelming presence inside of me. I knew it was my father, and tears came to my eyes as I experienced his feelings of pride that his daughter had written a book that would be published in his native tongue. It was a healing and wonderful experience that I will always treasure.

Not all visitations, visions, or signs have to be dramatic, of course. Larry's story is one of a soft awakening, where psychic ability blossomed as he aged and let him be open to experiencing the reality that his father was still very much alive in the realm of spirit.

Sometimes a person will sense the deceased through just a gentle nudging. Julie (not her real name) wrote that her mother "helped me pick out my dress and accessories for her funeral, literally. The earrings that matched the dress fell off of the rack, onto the floor, so I would have to pick them up. A song came on in the department store that we had talked about being a good song for the funeral. When I heard the song, I turned around, and there was the dress.

"After her death I experienced her almost in a dream state. I understood how difficult it was for her to see us suffer over her loss; that was the hardest for her. She was in a very good place."

Signs like Julie received (an object that falls unexplainably on the floor, meaningful music that comes on just when you need it) are very often reported by people who have lost someone dear to them. Of course these signs could be excused away as coincidences. But I don't believe that. Why? Because the people who receive these signs change. They are comforted. They are motivated. They become part of the elder generation.

Sometimes, receiving psychic information can lead to an emotional recovery or even a reuniting of relationships. Terese tells this story of how her life changed after receiving a reading from me.

"During the summer of 2007, I had a reading with Kathryn Harwig. It was during the reading that Kathryn shared with me that a family member of mine was having serious health issues. Not knowing which family member and being estranged from my family, I had my work cut out for me. I desperately wanted to reconnect with my family should the outcome be death, but was very unsure about contacting any of them. Shortly after our reading, Kathryn called me back with a message from my brother Troy that gave me just enough courage to make the first move. Because Troy and I were close at one period in my life, and with the intuitive message Kathryn gave me, I left Troy a message at his work and at his home. In just a short time, Troy returned my call. We talked on the phone and set a date to meet. It was good to see Troy; it had been way too long.

"I was feeling hopeful of being reunited with the rest of my family and set my intentions on reuniting with my sister, Teri. I left Teri a message with a phone number to reach back to me and she did. She was polite. Short. Asked nothing and shared nothing. Her phone number came up 'Private' and she offered no cell number. She indicated that she would have to look at her calendar for availability to see me. She would get back to me. She called a few days later at about eleven a.m. Yes, she had time to lunch that day, and if I couldn't make it she understood. I was living at least an hour away and at work. We didn't lunch. With that typical cold response from my sister, I gave up my quest to find the family member with serious health issues. I again felt like I was not part of the family.

"One month later, my brother Tom died of a massive heart attack. There were so many lessons in that experience but the one I honor the most is…trusting intuition."

While Terese's story doesn't (yet) have the perfect happy ending she desired, it does illustrate some wonderful lessons about intuition. Terese acted on the message she received. She reached out to her family and was able to speak to some of them. She opened a door to the healing I am sure will come if she lets it. Terese's story also illustrates how allowing our emotions to get in the way of intuition (in this case, Terese's feelings of being rejected) stands in the way of acting on our intuitive knowing. As Terese so wisely points out, knowing *and* acting on our intuition will make our lives better.

Sometimes, we receive a sign or a dream as a way to provide closure. Mary Ann tells of a dream that allowed her husband to move on after his father's death.

"About a month after my father-in-law died in September of 2008, my husband said he had had a dream in which his siblings were told that Dad was trying to get a message to him. I asked him if he got the message and he said no. So, wouldn't you know it, I received the message the next night. In my dream I saw my father-in-law fishing off a dock. (In his life on earth, he loved fishing.) I said to my husband, 'Let's go see your Dad.' We got into a rowboat and went near the dock. His dad looked very well and young and was enjoying his fishing. We didn't speak to him or him to us, but we simply watched him from the boat and I smiled at my husband. When I woke up I told him the dream and asked if he thought that was the message his dad wanted him to know, that he was well and fishing. My husband said yes. I think he was surprised that the dream came to me and not him, even though he's used to my dreams being more vivid and weird. Neither one of us has had a dream about his dad since, so I think it was a message for some kind of closure."

Some of the closest relationships many of us have are to non-humans. Our pets are incredibly important to us, especially as we age. Many of my respondents report that they have a nonverbal communication with their animal companions. We not only have the ability to psychically communicate with our pets when they are with us, but they also often visit us after they die. These messages of hope from our loving companions help us deal with the grief.

Brad tells of the death of his beloved dog three years ago. He writes: "Three weeks after putting my dog down, as I was awakening one morning, I saw her light body. It was just like her physical body, including all detail with movement and full eye contact. We had a conversation with our eyes. I knew why she was there. She had come back to comfort me. We, like most pets and their owners, had a very special bond. I know she also wanted me to come out and play with her as she turned to go down the stairway and then faded away."

Many people have reported to me that their deceased animals continue to visit them, offering comfort and hope, and acting as a sort of guide for them. This does not surprise me. Love doesn't die, no matter what body we most recently inhabited.

nine

....

Divorce, Job Loss, and Other Life Lessons

Unfortunately, it often takes a major event to get our attention, usually one that is not initially viewed as positive. Many of those who responded to my survey told me that things like a job loss, a divorce, or a physical move triggered their latent psychic abilities to emerge.

For twenty-five years, Joni worked as a recreation therapist with clients suffering from schizophrenia. She knew that her intuition helped her to do this job, or as she puts it, "After many years of putting the pieces of the puzzle together to help them, it seemed like I was really feeling what they were going through and could easily guess at the scenarios that were troubling them—and I was usually right."

After budget cuts, she was laid off. She started her own business, helping people with major mental illness to live in the community, working in the same way she had done at the mental health center. She goes on to say: "I worked long, hard hours, but I really became like a family member and 'knew' my clients really well. I did that for three years while I continued to study holistic techniques with the intention of starting my own business to help people heal themselves. After three years in my own business, and twenty-seven years in the mental health field, I was *tired*. I closed that business and started helping others heal themselves."

Joni used her layoff as a motivator in her life. First she started her own mental health business, but soon realized that doing the same thing got her the same result. And that result was to be tired. Unwilling to live that way, she started studying other ways of healing and helping people.

Today Joni works as a healer and the more she does this, the more her psychic abilities grow. She describes it like this: "When I do 'balancing' with people, to help them get their energy back into balance through different techniques, I use applied kinesiology or muscle checking when asking their systems what they need to shift their energy to a new level. While I'm working with them, and I'm touching their arm to muscle check, the questions I need to ask of them pop into my head. I can usually feel what their answers will be before I muscle check."

Intuition not only helped Joni find a new (non-tiring) vocation, it also helps her in her day-to-day life. As she says, "I have things pop into my head, it feels like thoughts or ideas, and I usually dismiss them, only to find a few minutes to a few hours later that I realize why it popped into my head. I am now trying to pay more attention to my thoughts and knowing, and acknowledge and act on them more quickly than before."

That is what getting psychic information feels like. It is, simply put, information that just pops into your head. What makes it psychic is that it is valuable, useful information that you could not get by ordinary means or through your regular senses. The key, as Joni says so well, is to listen to it and act upon it.

Laurie, too, had an awakening after a layoff. She wrote: "A take-over of my executive position in January of 2008, and the opportunity to leave that organization with severance pay, gave me time to just *be* and be silent.

"I traveled to Sedona, Arizona, at the end of March with my family, but returned by myself in mid April. It was all about just *being* and not *doing*. While I was there, a shaman appeared to me and has now set me on the path of healing.

"Since March I've traveled to Sedona six times and have monthly trips planned. I've lost seventy pounds, I have a new job, I'm in the midst of writing a book on spiritual leading, and I'm divorcing my husband.

While I started a new corporate job on June 1, my plan is to leave the corporate world sometime within the next three years to live in Arizona."

As can be seen, Laurie made major changes in her life. These changes, which she sees as very positive, were prompted first by her layoff and then fostered by her period of retreat, solitude, and, as she puts it, "just being." This time of being and introspection allowed Laurie to find her intuitive voice, which then aided her in creating a whole new life.

When Brad was suddenly laid off from his job as a radio personality, he felt he had not merely lost a vocation, he had lost an identity. At age fifty-seven, he was not only thrown into a difficult job market, but he lost his friends, a job he loved, and a way to express his creativity. He grieved not only the loss of a paycheck but also his contact with his radio audience.

Although he says it is "too early to tell" what the effect of this layoff will be, he does sense that it has prompted an "increase in his intuitive ability and capacity."

A family crisis also can act as a trigger for psychic ability. Shelli told me: "The event that threw me into a higher state of awareness about myself was my sixteen-year-old daughter running away from home and becoming a pregnant, homeless addict. This event in my life awoke a level of understanding about how the world worked, and I immediately fell into a mode of positive thinking, prayer, and absolute knowing that my grandchild and daughter would be fine. My psychic abilities led me to find her several times, in areas of town no one should go. The story is a long one...but my daughter and her children are healthy, happy, and alive!"

Since that time, Shelli continued, "I have opened myself up to the energy, and since I have it's been pouring in like Niagara Falls. I hear things, see people, and know things without knowing. I can zero in on a person's soul purpose and help them with their own inner development. I just know—the person does not have to be in front of me to do this. I have spoken to relatives and heard stories of strangers...on and on. The more I do this, the stronger it gets."

Shelli makes several good points. Once psychic ability is opened up, it is difficult to shut down. And, like all skills, the more we use it, the better we get at it.

Not all wake-up calls result in quite such dramatic life changes as did Laurie's and Shelli's, but many of them prompt the person to take a look at their life, and as Laurie says, just *be* for a while.

Some of the triggers happen slowly and over time. Kathy told me that "During my twenties and thirties I was too busy playing and having too much fun (or what was fun then) to allow it (intuition) to surface. Then, in my forties and now fifties I am really enjoying exploring and utilizing my rediscovered intuitiveness."

She goes on to say: "For over fifteen years I bred and showed prize-winning French bulldogs. I also wrote a book on them that was published by Howell (now Wiley) books, and started a French bulldog magazine, for which I did the design and layout for four years.

I lived, breathed, and slept French bulldogs. Then a series of what someone else might have viewed as 'bad luck' events happened to me within my Frenchie world, and I made the gut-wrenching decision to quit showing and breeding them. It was as if my entire identity had been tied up in these sweet little dogs, and I was devastated ... but I *knew* I could not turn back. My stepping away from such an all-consuming passion opened the doors to my exploration and rediscovering of my intuitive abilities and interests."

Today, Kathy describes herself like this: "It is as if my senses became finer tuned. I allowed myself to *feel* more and to listen to that small voice within. I lost that competitiveness that had driven me for so many years and *relaxed*. I just *knew* things, I could pick up on people's feelings much more readily and I literally felt myself becoming kinder and more open. I also consciously worked on *not* being judgmental of others ... a deeply ingrained pattern."

Kathy's story illustrates a common theme told to me by the respondents. Often the most devastating of events (the loss of a loved one, a job, health, etc.) is later viewed by the person as a trigger to a whole new and wonderful intuitive life.

Seemingly small events can bring huge changes into our lives and the lives of others. Carolyn tells of just another day in her job that changed her life.

She wrote: "Many things have happened in my life, but a pivotal time was the day I was working in suicide prevention and was driving in my car to five different sheriff and police departments. It was a very hot and exhausting day. It was four p.m., and I had a two-hour drive to get home, with still another stop to make along the way.

"Up until this point in my life I had a lot of doubts about what or who was guiding me. So, when I got the (psychic) message that I needed to make this stop, I argued with it and then said to myself, 'This better be worth the time and energy because I would just like to cancel this visit and head home.'

"I went to this appointment at a law enforcement center in a small town. This was the only department where the chief didn't want to see me directly. In fact, I was never allowed access to him. The next person in line insisted I meet with him instead.

"That day I entered the building, was buzzed in, and the officer I was to meet with let me in and we met in the lobby. No one was around, which was strange for a late afternoon. I still asked for the chief and was sternly told that he wasn't available. So, I gave the officer all the information I had on how to prevent suicide in their community, what my role would be, and some community resources lists.

"While I was doing this, a man came into the room and stood at the doorway. I noticed right away that the officer I was visiting with became nervous at his presence. The gentleman never looked at me, but just stood in the door and listened to me talk about suicide prevention.

"All of a sudden, I felt this sense of someone being with me ... the same sense I had experienced in my car. It felt like a very persistent young person.

"Oddly, at that moment, the man in the door spoke to me, 'I know what it feels like to have someone commit suicide,' he said, with his head down. He looked as though he was doing everything he could to prevent himself from going to his knees.

"Immediately I was told what to say. 'Sir, your son didn't end his life because he thought you didn't love him. He was living in a fog and couldn't live with his own pain any longer.'

"He looked over to me and said, choking back the tears, 'I never told him I loved him. If only I had, maybe he wouldn't have done this. He did this with my gun. I should have seen this coming.'

"Then I knew why I was supposed to stop there and what this was all about. We visited. It turned out this was the chief, and his staff was trying to protect him from dealing with suicide prevention, as his son had ended his life nine months prior. The day ended with him carrying my things to my car, and we hugged goodbye.

"When I got into my car I sat for a while. Renewed ... at peace ... I got it. From that point on, I have been working quietly behind the scenes, using my gifts. It is now time to just be me."

That day changed how Carolyn viewed her life, her job, and her mission. It opened her up to believing in her inherent psychic abilities. And I am sure it helped to heal the grief that the chief was suffering.

Our intuition often leads us to jobs or volunteer opportunities where we can help other people as well as ourselves. Deb tells of "manifesting" a job as a hospice volunteer coordinator. This job allows her "to help journey along the end of life's path with many others." While other people might find the job depressing, Deb finds it a way to use her intuitive skills in the service of others. As she states: "The gift of service and providing presence to another as they journey at the end of life is a very rich and insightful experience. As a volunteer coordinator in hospice, I am continually approached by people who have a calling to volunteer and am able to work with these individuals to share what I have learned and serve them in their personal journey."

One of the gifts of aging is the opportunity and ability to share our wisdom with others. Deb and Carolyn are wonderful examples of how, by tapping into their intuition, they are also able to lighten the load carried by other people.

Sometimes, intuition can prepare us enough that we take precautions and prevent things from happening. Deborah, who says she has been intuitive all her life, credits psychic knowing for helping her keep a job during these tough economic times. She wrote: "I was told (intuitively) about a major possible bad job happening. This prompted me to move settings within my current job, so as to not be a part of the bad happenings that have occurred there in the last few years." That is the wonderful thing about intuition. If you heed it, it will provide warnings and information and help you prepare for, and hopefully avoid, crises of all kinds.

Sometimes it takes the loss of an identity, whether it be by a change or loss of employment or a change or loss of a relationship, to really get our attention and trigger our psychic ability.

Many of my respondents said that the major changes caused by a divorce opened up a whole new world of possibilities to them. Wendy describes it well: "In my mid-forties, around 2002, I felt like a real shift in my life's energy happened when suddenly, after a long time in an unhappy marriage, my now-ex husband decided he was ready to split up. It was like a gate opened and I was suddenly meeting all kinds of new people, the likes of which I had never connected to before. And, it seemed that with each one there was some connection, past-life or karmic lesson to be learned. Sometimes it was an energy that I felt I was to be in their lives and sometimes they had a lesson for me. Since then I've met *so* many people who feel that connection, too, and we understand so much more clearly that there are definite reasons, still unknown, for our meeting up with each other.

"My divorce released a lot of anger and I got back my spirit. It returned my freedom and got me away from all that bad energy."

Sometimes, our intuition also lets us know when it is time to leave a relationship we have outgrown. Vicki wrote, "I realized I was intuitive when a longtime relationship ended. I knew when he was talking to the other woman on the phone. I would call his number and it would be busy. I would call hers and it would be busy. When I did get through to him and told him I knew he was talking to her, he was flabbergasted. He thought I had his phone bugged."

Sometimes, even the worst of relationships contains the seed of growth. Literally hours after she married in 1972, Sheryl realized her husband was abusive. The emotional abuse escalated into physical abuse, including broken bones and other injuries. She wrote: "The emotional abuse's wounds were much deeper than my physical wounding. I was so astonished (by the abuse) that I really believed that if I was more loving, more patient, and more long suffering, it would go away. But it did not. I couldn't hide it anymore and divorced and moved away."

She goes on: "I looked and acted like a broken soul, hiding my eyes when I spoke, but also determined to unravel this experience." She began to write, study, and learn about spiritual things. Now, in her early fifties, she is happily remarried, a successful artist and business owner, and, as she describes herself, "Doing what I love to do each day, and my world is wonderful."

Luckily, not all awakenings are caused by traumatic or even dramatic occurrences. Sometimes, it is triggered by a lovely event such as a new love. Bobbie wrote that she "grew up in a very dysfunctional family and had very low self-esteem my entire life. I have never trusted myself and because of that have never been able to make decisions on my own." Then, three years ago, she met a man who "believed in me as a person and helped me get through the remnants of my harsh childhood."

She believes that this relationship has allowed her to open herself to her latent psychic abilities. She goes on to say: "My self-esteem is rising and I am learning to trust myself. It's almost as if when I made the decision to start trusting myself, more and more 'visions' seemed to be coming through. I have also found peace in my new life and become more introspective, and love reading and my quiet time."

For some, the circumstances of aging, having more time, and consciously desiring an awakening are all it takes. Mary had a dramatic vision of a dead cousin at age four (see chapter two), but then quashed her psychic ability because of religious fears. As she grew older, this quashing no longer made sense to her. She told me: "Once my three children got older and on their own, I was able to read all I could about angels and spiritual things. The more I read, the more spiritual I became. The more spiritual I became, the further away I got from religions. I would say that having time to meditate and read and learn on my own after the children grew older and moved out was the trigger to me learning about what I really believed about myself. I did not have to hide what I knew to be the truth."

This beautiful and gentle awakening is something that we all could strive to attain. Mary is happier, healthier, and helping others to be that way as well. She continues: "I have always been able to sort of know what people are feeling. I can pick up their emotions, and I know the vibes of a happy or unhappy place. Now, I see all of this as a blessing and a gift. I am no longer embarrassed to talk about this. I am much more open with my family and friends about these matters. I still have friends who I don't talk about this with, because I am afraid they will no longer like me, but ... I have come a long way."

For Rita, it all started by reading a book. She writes: "It all started in my early fifties. I can't remember how I stumbled on the book *We Don't Die*, but after reading it, it became the beginning of an exciting and intense spiritual journey. I was afraid of dying in my twenties, thirties, and forties, but after reading the book, I lost that fear. That made me think, 'maybe I am on to something here.'"

"I read every book I could get my hands on, including, but not limited to, those about psychics, mediums, out-of-body experiences, remote viewing, shamans, near death experiences, Native American spirituality, synchronicity, dreams, astral projection, telepathy, reincarnation, past life recall, auras, chakras, and many more. I just couldn't seem to fill my need to explore this new spiritual realm. Of course, I couldn't discuss what I was discovering and learning with my family or friends, except for my husband and a couple of friends. I didn't want anyone to think I was out of my mind. I suspected they wouldn't be able to accept these views of life, death, and communicating with spirits."

Rita continued, "After retiring at age sixty-five, I began to attend classes and workshops. I learned more about medical intuitives, animal communicators, tarot reading, past life regression, spirit guides, angels, chakras, and the energy of stones." Through taking classes, reading books, and attending lectures, Rita has grown and has had many intuitive experiences. This is how she describes her life today: "I feel like I'm on a never-ending adventure as I discover new spiritual energies. I feel so much closer to all things spiritual and to my creator. I have so much joy in my heart and am truly at peace with death. I only wish I could have had the opportunity to learn about spiritual things when I was younger. But, being brought up Catholic kept me from pursuing anything spiritual or supernatural. As I look back, I think my intuitiveness was awakened and working already when I was younger. I just didn't know it. This awakening has been such a gift to me, especially at this point in my life."

Cheri's awakening started on the back of a motorcycle. She wrote to say: "The universe works its magic in subtle ways. It's hard to know when exactly I became aware of my inherent psychic abilities."

She goes on: "Do all midlife crises start on a Harley? I had a friend who finally achieved her goal to get a bike, a Harley. She persuaded me to go riding with her biker friends. So, off we went through the Wisconsin countryside, and while all the discussion was about the joys of riding a bike, all I could see or say was, 'look at all the horses.'"

Seeing the horses brought Cheri back to lost child-hood dreams. Years later, Cheri found what she calls her "first great love" ... a horse named Casey. Through working with Casey, Cheri learned to become an animal communicator, a healer, and a psychic. She goes on: "My sense of wonder and yes, even my sense of gratefulness to the universe has increased. I am aware of what a great journey this life of mine has been and can be. With the magic of the universe I will continue to meet wonderful people and loving and teaching animal friends. Life is a great adventure. That still, small voice is talking to me, and it says, 'You go, girl!' At age sixty-four, it's only getting better."

Penny writes that her awakening is developing slowly as she ages. Although she admits to having many traumatic events earlier in her life (a serious illness, layoffs, and a depression), she says that, "It's only been in the last year or two that I have felt more and more that I am on a journey or a quest, yet available religions in the areas I grew up and subsequently lived in have left me feeling lost."

She continues, saying, "Now, in the last year or two I am listening to my 'soul mind' and paying more attention to the feelings that I have about certain things in my life. These seem to be even stronger since I've been trying to focus on being positive and joyful. I feel strongly with a more certain 'knowing' that I *am* creating what it is I want in my life."

Mary describes her emerging intuition in this way: "It's still developing. (I'm not fifty until next year.) I get intuitive feelings about people. The name of someone I know but hadn't seen or thought of in a while will come into my mind. I can't pin down the feeling to know exactly what it means at that moment, but very often, sometime soon afterward, I'll get a phone call or hear from a friend or relative that someone close to me (but not living nearby) is ill or has lost their job, for example. I 'heard' a coworker's name one weekend, just randomly, and the next day back at the office I found out she had just been laid off. I was recently at an evening work event where prizes were given away, and I played a game with myself trying to *feel* whose name would be called to win. I clearly heard the name of a woman whom I knew, and hers was the next name called! I laughed to myself, not surprised at all by it. I once won a trip at an event by correctly knowing three cards in a deck (I had to pick one to match the displayed card and I was right three times). So sometimes I pick up a deck of cards and try to guess which one is on top."

Mary's "games," as she calls them, are really a very good example of practicing and honing psychic ability. Like all abilities, intuition gets stronger and more reliable the more you use it. This practice is certain to aid her as she advances into her place as an elder.

I tell my students that one way you will know psychic ability is real is that your life gets better when you use it. These stories illustrate in a touching way the real advantage of being in the elder generations. Your life becomes an adventure. You intuitively know what to do. Your inner voice and wisdom allow you to aid other people. And ... it only gets better.

ten

....

Advice for Family and Friends

After being opened to the psychic world, either by a dramatic and often traumatic event, or more gently as a soft awakening, a person is irrevocably changed. Often, they crave more solitude and draw away from their friends and family. This is particularly true if the family and friends respond to the change with criticism, doubt, and ridicule. Of course, this causes their loved ones to be confused and perhaps afraid. It sometimes causes a cycle of confusion, distrust, and withdrawal between the family and the older relative or friend.

Bob came to see me after his aunt Sally (names have been changed) moved in with him and his wife. Even though Sally was in her late eighties, she was alert and physically able, although a little frail. What concerned him was that she talked to herself and often seemed to be having conversations with her dead husband and other relatives and friends in spirit.

"What," Bob asked me, "can we do to bring her out of this?" I laughed. My response was perhaps not what he wanted to hear. "Bob," I replied. "How do you know Aunt Sally is *not* talking to her dead husband? Just because you can't see or hear him doesn't mean she can't."

Often, well-meaning friends and family urge older people to get out more, and to snap out of it. Well, some of us don't want to snap. We are pleased that we are becoming mystics and seers. As an increasing number of people reach their fifties and beyond, it is becoming even more important that their loved ones support them, even if it is outside of their own personal comfort level and belief system.

One of the questions in my survey was: "Have you noticed any changes in the way your friends and/or family treat you since you developed these awakened abilities?"

People handle changes in their loved ones in many different ways, particularly when it comes to intuitive experiences or spirit communication. As Pam put it: "Sometimes they seem to sidestep around me, and that is very unusual for me, but these are friends who maybe have had other agendas for me. Part of my family likes it, the other side tells me that I am crazy. A few like to scare me away from it. And some say I made the whole thing up."

Carolyn answered: "They sometimes make jokes and poke fun. Other times, they seem to be contemplating what is really going on, but not with fear. They are curious but cautious. Interested but don't want to go *there*."

In some ways, it is not surprising that her family is reacting with fear and caution. As Carolyn goes on to describe, "I have become less tolerant of hanging with people I never really liked—I just don't care to pretend anymore. Having things appear and disappear is getting old and tiring—I am certain that much of it isn't because I'm getting forgetful. Rather, something else seems to be involved. Forgetfulness? Oh my…so many things do not seem worth remembering anymore. I am frustrated that I don't seem to pay much attention to making sure about the who, what, when, and where as I used to."

For many of us, aging ushers in a natural pulling away from things and people that used to matter to us. We may find ourselves no longer interested in hosting those large family gatherings as we have done for years. We get tired of going to the same places and seeing the same people. The pull of spirit and intuition gets stronger.

It is, in my opinion, important to support your aging friends and family in their retreat from the ordinary. Recognize they are entering a new era. Be excited for them when they pull away. Ask them to describe what is happening and then, of course, don't make fun of it. Becoming a sage and a mystic is the natural way of aging. Help them to rejoice in their new-found abilities and interests rather than discounting them.

Many respondents told me that they simply *can't* talk about their experiences to many people. As Cheryl says: "They give me a pretty bad time about it—that is, the family that knows about it. My kids think it is kind of funny. As far as friends, my best friend is having a hard time with this. She has very strong Christian beliefs so I have had to tread lightly with her. She understands energy and things like that but draws the line at talking to dead people and reincarnation. I can tell that she gets uncomfortable if I talk about things like this."

Penny says: "Friends seem more distant to me, and I don't feel like I have friends, just friendly acquaintances. One close friend remains, and we've discovered she is on a similar journey. We have found things in common, so I have at least one person to talk with. My husband has always been my best friend, but I cannot talk to him—he doesn't want to hear what I want to talk about. It's not that he won't listen if I say something, but there is no return conversation. He says he feels I've become more distant, not the other way around. My daughters are somewhat accepting, my son and other family members are not. In a recent visit with a brother, when I tried to explain what I was feeling and how I was believing I was creating my life, he ridiculed me and my husband joined in, which saddened me. I don't have the right words to explain to others what I'm feeling."

Since part of the aging process is becoming more psychic, we can intuitively tell if someone does not wish to hear what is really going on with us. So, we become quiet. If you find that an aging loved one or friend is pulling away from you, you might wish to ask yourself if you are making fun of him or her, or refusing to talk about topics that make *you* uncomfortable.

Terri describes what it feels like: "I have learned not to discuss some of my experiences with those friends and family members who seem uncomfortable with psychic events—they aren't ready. Others who are unsure might be open to hearing what I know and I'll share with them, but I find myself being most candid with those who acknowledge psychic phenomena— and I like nothing better than sharing and learning with them."

Many of us have learned to shut up around people who don't understand. As Kim says, "They (her family) know something is going on with me, but they never ask. Most of the time I am happy with this, but once in a while it frustrates me that no one does ask. The stand I've taken and don't plan to change is that if you don't ask, I don't tell."

Brad echoes this theme. He said: "Most of my family members do not understand the other information or greater awareness that has evolved in my life from these turning points. Only a few kindred family members and friends seem to truly understand the larger picture and greater context of this personal transformation and new awareness."

Dee describes it similarly: "I only share strange things that have happened with one friend and my daughter, Heidi. They think like I do, while others are great doubters, and think I am strange, or losing it!"

Lisa said almost the same thing: "I try not to discuss it too much because I know they think it is weird. My sister and my mom listen but don't say too much—even though they have had experiences too."

Mary used nearly the same words: "Sometimes I think my daughter and some of my siblings think I am losing it! They feel I am off in my own little world. My husband is supportive, but is much more into day-to-day activities than I am. I feel a pull toward something bigger, and I'm not sure what that is."

Nobody likes to be thought of as losing it, or to be considered weird. It is as if we have had a conspiracy of silence in which the natural psychic abilities that come with aging have become a forbidden topic of conversation. Few of us have the courage to tell our doctor or minister or even family that we are spending quality time with a spirit, or that we are getting messages from birds. It is easier to pull away, pretend to watch television, or read. No wonder so many aging people feel more comfortable in solitude. Breaking this boundary of silence is one of the main reasons I decided to write this book.

If we don't pull away, then we can always just pretend. Joanie describes her way of coping: "Now I live in two worlds. I have the world where I can be open, honest, and happy with my friends of like mind. Where I can ask questions about things I don't understand and I can share experiences without someone commenting that I belong in a hospital. Then I have the other group; it is the group of friends and relatives where I need to guard what I say in their presence. I have been ridiculed, criticized, and prayed for by the second group of friends and relatives. It has been such a struggle to let go of the old friends, or the relatives that think you are someone that fell off the looney bin. I am getting better with it now. I just play the game and don't say anything. The weather is always a good, safe topic! At family gatherings I sit quietly and wait until it is time to leave. When I meet a new person, I can pretty well sum up what I will share with them quickly. If I hear one comment about religion, I know to be quiet."

Pretending to be someone we are not takes its toll. As a family member, watch the older people at your gatherings. Are they sitting there, waiting to leave? Are they avoiding all but safe topics like the weather? Perhaps, like Joanie, they are just not able to tell you the truth about what is going on in their lives.

If you are a relative or friend of someone like Joanie, consider this: If they are pulling away from you, it may be because you do not "listen and believe." An open mind is a terrible thing to waste. The information they are receiving may be just what you need to hear.

Sadly, some of these elders are even being shunned by their family and former friends. Roberta told me: "Most of the time I feel invisible. I know for sure one of my brothers does not want me around his two daughters (ages ten and twelve) because I will answer their questions about spirits and he thinks it is all nonsense."

It is tragic that Roberta's nieces are not allowed to benefit from her wisdom. It is a sad example of how the experiences and knowledge of the aged in our society are not honored. It is hard to fathom all the lost wisdom and psychic information that is not shared, just because no one cared to listen.

Some families completely abandon those who don't act the way they want them to or believe what they believe. Laurie told me that after she spoke of her psychic experiences her "family and my partner's family have basically said 'Adios.'" Wendy said, "Any discussion with my siblings about these well-known family experiences now results in being shunned or dismissed as never happening." Vanette says: "People are scared of me because things just start coming out of my mouth in conversation and I will end up striking a deep chord with someone without even knowing it."

It is lonely not be able to talk about our true experiences. As Stephanie puts it, "I have primarily kept these things to myself, since they're a little offbeat and my friends/family are very mainstream."

The lucky (and brave) ones sometimes find the inner courage to continue their journey, even when they have no support. Dar says: "At first, those whom I would call my family were disdainful, distant, and mocking. It was very hurtful. I struggled to come to terms with this and when I did—exactly when I did—everything around me shifted. It was incredible. I am now respected, not for what I believe (I stopped talking about that a long time ago), but for who I am. I'm not perfect by any means, but even being able to embrace that holds such meaning for me."

How wonderful it would have been for Dar, though, if she had been able to come to that place surrounded by people who *did* support her and if she could indeed talk about her beliefs and experiences.

Since we can't talk to many of our family members and friends, some elders are creating a new family with peers and others who are learning the same life lessons. The need for a community of like minds is critical. Older people who are having psychic experiences don't need psychiatrists or medication to help cure us of our visions and unusual thoughts. What we need is support and understanding and a community of people who understand what is happening to us. We need our visions honored and our dreams shared. We need support and community in equal measure.

Even the act of filling out the questionnaire was a way of finding community for some of the respondents. Bobbie wrote how she found out about me and this book. "This is my first step in trying to understand and learn more. I was watching a show about psychics and how they help police investigations and Kathryn Harwig was featured on the show and said things that I was looking for answers to. I almost cried when I started reading things on this website that made sense to me."

I was touched by Bobbie's comments. Many people feel so alone in their psychic ability that even a person on television or in a book will allow them to feel less alone. It is my strong hope that this book will prompt you, as a reader, to feel a part of the growing and vital community of elders.

Of course, not all of us feel isolated. Some of us have been lucky to find support with our peers. Sheryl says: "I spend time with people who encourage me, have the same experiences and knowingness, and listen to that still, small voice that has been talking to me for years." Wendy adds: "I tend to have more intuitive friends. I definitely spend less time with people who are not positive and who are judgmental about things and other people." Carole adds: "I have a select group of family and friends who listen and believe. Others do not speak of the situation."

Some of us have had to make dramatic changes in our lives in order to feel this support and community. Peggy tells of leaving her husband and moving to a new community, where she found friends who supported her on this journey.

As she put it, "It seemed as if I no longer had any of the same interests as my friends, so we grew apart. I moved away without my husband. I wanted to move and he didn't. My family didn't understand this. It was unusual to live apart and created some discomfort with my parents and some siblings. My children were very supportive and helpful. They were confused at times because I had raised them in a certain way and taught them certain things and now my beliefs were changing and I was teaching them new ways."

Peggy's move changed her enough that a few years later she felt confident to return to her husband and former home. Today, she is creating her perfect life, secure in her own psychic abilities and yet adapting to her new and better life.

Like Peggy, many of us have taken these experiences, acted upon them, changed our lives, and are now living productive and fruitful stage-three lives. Teri says: "My family has been supportive for the most part, however it can be a struggle because they don't get it and it is so huge I can't even explain it. Friends I have met through this have gathered around me and a business is falling into place around my abilities. I have a manager/partner, a marketing representative, people involved with healing, etc. All of these pieces are falling into place around me without going after it myself. So many believe in me more than I do in myself. It is so phenomenal!"

One of the themes of the elder generation is echoed in Teri's story. When our friends and families don't or won't "get it," we need to form our support system from those who do.

Of course, there are the lucky ones, the people whose families rejoice with them and whose friends want to know, "What happened and how can I get some?"

Laurie joyously writes: "They all notice a change and say I'm glowing, sparkling, or have a twinkle in my eye and a bounce in my step, and they *want some!*" Re-nay says that her psychic development has brought her even closer to her daughter. She says: "We just seem to know when we need to call each other." Kathy writes: "They *love it*! I am kinder and more open with people. I hug more, I tell them I love them more, geesh, *I like myself* more—so no wonder they enjoy me more."

Having loving and supportive family members makes all the difference. Of course, as members of the elder generation, we also need to give our loved ones time and space and understanding as they learn to deal with our changes. Listen to how gently Linda describes how her family accepts her new abilities: "My mother laughs at me in a loving way. She is just on a different path, I believe. My daughters say, 'See, we told you.' They very much believe in everything I've told them. I do have good friends that I can talk to about my para-normal experiences. There is one in particular—with-out her in the beginning days of my vibrations and vi-sions, I don't know what I would have done. She was right there for me and told me what books to read. Although we both were perplexed about my vibra-tions and what they were, I just knew when I started to feel them, I was gonna go somewhere. I just had to *see* where."

Some family members and friends go so far as to joyously embrace the skills. Shelly tells us: "Friends want readings from me on a regular basis, they bring me their mothers, questions, dreams. They want to speak to the other side…on and on." John had the same experience. He wrote: " It does seem that once my family found out about me, they couldn't wait to have a reading or something special for them."

Often, the most accepting families are those in which many of the elders are psychic. Ann tells us: "My family is quite open and I find a wonderful mentor in my older brother. My family has many psychic gifts, and only now are we open and exploring them." As Kay puts it: "It seemed to run in my mother's side of the family and was embraced (somewhat secretly). I feel I am getting increasingly more intuitive and joyful as I reach my fifties."

As these gifts become accepted by society, more families like Ann's and Kay's will be open to passing on their inherent abilities to the next generation. Just as physical strength, musical talent, or many other gifts can be hereditary, so too is natural psychic ability. While all of these talents need practice and focus to become perfected, some families do have natural inherent psychic ability. What a marvelous legacy to pass on to your grandchildren and to honor in your grandparents.

As family members, wouldn't you rather have your parents, grandparents, and other relatives intuitively knowing when to call you and walking around with a bounce in their step and a twinkle in their eyes? Can you learn to laugh lovingly, even when you don't understand?

You can help by being open, by encouraging them to find and develop their intuition, and by aiding them to see that this new stage in life may be the richest and fullest time ever. Then, when your time comes (and come it will) you will have a rich model of how to live the final third of your life with dignity, vision, and intuitive wisdom.

eleven

Where Do We Go from Here?

By now you have read dozens of stories written by people who have either suddenly, due to a life change, or slowly, by a gentle awakening, started to blossom into their psychic heritage. Perhaps you are able to relate to many of their stories. You may also be wondering where you can go from here.

Many of the stories thus far involved psychic events and spirit visitations that happened to the person spontaneously. It is how most people believe psychic events happen to them. I call it the "drive-by shooting" approach to intuition. You are just standing around and *boom*, you are hit with it.

This is the way in which many of us have experienced psychic events, at least at first. After a taste though, of the incredible things intuition has to offer, many of us wish to take that ability and turn it into something we can use. We want to take control of these events and make them usable, predictable, and most of all, valuable to us.

My book *The Intuitive Advantage* details many exercises and methods you can use to turn intuitive ability into a tool at your command. I won't go into detail about this information as it is easily obtainable for those who are interested. I do, however, highly recommend reading a few books and taking a course or two on intuitive techniques.

In my opinion, everyone would benefit from mastering their intuition, regardless of their age. For those of us in midlife and beyond, however, there is a vast incentive to hone our psychic ability into a usable tool that will benefit both us and the world. It is time, I believe, for our generation to step forward and use our psychic gifts, not necessarily as a power source of money or knowledge, but as a well of mystical and spiritual resources to leave to and teach the next generation.

Here are some of the steps I urge you to consider. Doing these things will not necessarily *make* you a psychic, but it will set the stage so that your natural abilities will have a comfortable and easy place to grow. It is rather like gardening. You have the seeds of psychic ability deep inside of you. The following suggestions are equivalent to preparing a rich loamy soil, and then adding fertilizer and water and the warmth of the sun.

The growth of your intuition will occur naturally and peacefully in such an environment.

COME OUT OF THE CLOSET

Eleanor Roosevelt once said, "No one can make you feel inferior without your consent." I agree. No one can make you feel crazy without your consent either.

Part of taking back our intuitive power is refusing to allow others to define our beliefs for us. I have heard hundreds of tales from people who have had amazing experiences, only to end the story by saying, "And I can't tell anyone about this without sounding crazy."

It is not benefiting the world for us to pretend we are not talking to spirits, having psychic flashes, and knowing things without knowing how we know them. We are the sages, the mystics, the seers. It is time for us to start acting like it.

Start by telling your stories and owning your truth. It isn't necessary to get on a bandwagon and proclaim it to the world. Just quietly and with integrity refuse to hide anymore. If someone asks you how you know a thing, tell them the truth. Smile more. Refuse to go to parties that aren't fun. Sit in quiet confidence, secure in the knowledge that life lasts forever and that wisdom comes from the inside.

Our society has become much more accepting of differences than it was even twenty years ago. The bravery of gay individuals who proudly spoke their truth has made a profound difference in how the world views people of different sexual orientations. Now, it is our turn. We can use their coming out as a model for how we can proudly proclaim who *we* are without apologizing or explaining.

CHOOSE COURAGE

Erica Jong once said, "Courage is an acquired taste, like caviar." The first time someone told me I was courageous, I laughed out loud. I was perhaps the most timid child ever born on this planet. Partly due to my childhood illness and partly because of my peculiar psychic abilities, I didn't act like other children. I didn't play sports, never learned to ride a bike, and was afraid to go into the water. I stayed to myself, reading, pondering, and talking to spirits. And, I was afraid…a lot.

I remember the conscious decision I made to quit being afraid. I was perhaps sixteen at the time and I realized that I could live in fear for the rest of my life or I could develop courage. It was one of those moments of clarity when I realized that I could stay the way I was, or I could become who I wanted to be.

The thing with choosing courage is that it *does* grow on you. Each time I choose to do something outside of my comfort zone, it is easier than the time before. Not that I am not still afraid on occasion, but acting courageously does become a habit. I also believe that it helps others to do the same. As Marianne Williamson so eloquently said, "Your playing small does not serve the world."

If there is one personality characteristic that is required to be a psychic, it is courage. Faith without works may be dead, but so is intuition without action. Getting psychic information is one thing, but acting on that knowledge takes a leap of courage.

I have trained thousands of people in developing their intuitive skills. All people have these, but for most people they are left latent and unused. Learning a few techniques to tap your inner knowledge is fairly easy. What is more difficult is to take that knowing and use it in your own life. That is where courage comes to play.

The world is much more accepting of psychics than it was twenty years ago, but it still takes courage to follow your gut and your intuition, even when you can't consciously explain why you are doing so.

The thing about acting on your intuition is that when you do so you may not get proof that you were right. For example, perhaps you take the same route to work every morning. Then one morning you wake up with a strong intuitive sense that you should drive another way. If you have courage, you will follow your intuition and get to work safely and on time. Then, of course, you will never know what would have happened had you taken your normal route.

For example, not long ago I agreed to speak at an event held quite some distance away. I had made this commitment months before, but as the event approached I was told, in ever-increasing volume, not to go to the event. The day before it was scheduled, I was almost sick with anxiety. Do I break my word and disappoint the organizers and attendees, or do I disregard what is truly a strong and clear message of advice? Perhaps I would have felt better if I had heard, "If you go, you will get in an accident." Or even, "If you go, it will not go well." But intuition usually doesn't speak that way, at least for me. I just heard, "Don't go." Then it was up to me to decide what to do about it.

So there I was, being asked to speak on the topic of intuition and being a teacher who tells her students to follow their intuition. Yet I was tearing myself up inside because I just couldn't do that and let people down.

Still, in the end, I decided to cancel my participation. The organizers weren't happy, I felt horribly guilty, and I never received a bit of further feedback from my intuition as to why I should not have gone.

Would I do the same thing again? Well, yes, I certainly hope so. I will never know if I would have died in a car accident, said something to someone they shouldn't hear, or gotten ill. That is the thing with psychic information. We don't always get the stories that add explanation to our gut feelings, intuitive knowings, or telepathic rumblings.

So, many of us ignore our intuitive hits and take our usual routes. Then, when we get into an accident, we are able to say, "I *knew* I should have gone a different way." We now have a good story to tell about intuition.

Deborah tells a story that illustrates what happens when we *don't* act on our intuition. She wrote: "When my middle daughter was seventeen years old, she and her boyfriend were going to the mall to shop for the day. When I awoke that morning, my mind said to tell her not to go. This sense was so strong that I had major anxiety over it and did not understand it. I thought that if I told her she couldn't go she'd be so mad at me because I did not know why she shouldn't go. It took all my strength to not lock her in her closet for the rest of the day. Boy, did that seem crazy to me, but it was what I really wanted to do. I let her go, with dread in my heart. My day went on,. I let it go. At 10:25 p.m. that evening, I got a call from her boyfriend's parents that they were coming to pick me up. Something had happened—there had been an accident. My daughter sustained a head injury (but healed very quickly). Since that time, I've told my children that if I ever call and tell you not to do something, please listen."

Deborah learned the hard way. If you get an intuitive hit and don't act on it, you get a good story. The thing is, if you trust your intuition *and* act upon it, you tend to have fewer good stories and a better life. Now that you are an elder, you have permission to release your need to be right and have the courage to act on your inner knowing, even without verification. Your life will get better.

As William James put it, "If you want a quality, act as if you already had it." In the case of intuitive living, this means acting as if your hunches, feelings, and gut reactions are true and accurate. They are, of course, but our lack of confidence keeps us from believing that fact and then acting upon our inner knowing.

Judy told me a simple and yet very important example of the practical use of intuition. She wrote, "One morning while driving to work, I had a flash vision of someone crossing in a crosswalk near where I was driving, where people don't usually cross. When I got to that crosswalk, I had slowed down because of the vision, and lo and behold, someone actually was crossing in the crosswalk. It is possible that if I had been less careful, I could have hurt that person. (I don't want to make it sound like I was driving recklessly! But still, having someone cross in that area was very unexpected, especially at that hour of the morning.)"

Judy's example is powerful because of its simplicity. We don't always need huge and dramatic messages or visions in order to prevent an accident or save a life. What we need to do is listen to our intuition and act upon it.

There are such gifts that come with being elders. One is the freedom to act the way we wish. We don't need anyone else to verify for us that we are psychic. There is no need to wait for scientific proof of the validity of intuition. Do we wait to feel love just because it cannot be scientifically proven?

Some people believe that intuitive knowing must be 100 percent accurate. If you hold yourself to that standard (for anything in life), you will never act. Nothing is 100 percent accurate. Even if the knowing you receive is totally accurate, your interpretation of it might not be. Don't let that stand in the way of your trusting and using your psychic ability.

The more you act as if you are a psychic, the more you will realize the truth of it.

FOSTER YOUR SOLITUDE

Being busy is something in which we all take pride, at least in the United States. When I ask people how they are, they often answer, "Busy." I know I do that myself. This is true regardless of age, income bracket, sex, or nationality. It is a badge of honor. Even our small children have busy schedules. If we have a "hole" in our day, we seem compelled to fill it. Solitude and contemplation are unheard of in most people's lives. No wonder our psychic messages and our spirit friends have to yell so loudly to get our attention. It is no surprise we often ignore it or simply do not even hear it. Our intuition speaks best to us in a quiet, stress-free environment.

As we age, our bodies naturally wish to slow down. Things just take longer. I have retired friends who tell me, with a proud smile, that they are busier than they have ever been. I am not impressed. One of the great gifts of aging is time to think, rest, and listen to our intuition.

Almost every one of my respondents told me that they had noticed an increased desire to spend time alone as they aged. One person described it well. She called it a "settling of myself. I have less need to be overly involved. My family comments that I seem quieter."

By age fifty or so, most of us have paid our dues. Our children are grown and (hopefully) out of our houses. Our careers have likely settled down. Much of the frantic activity that is necessary for a person in their thirties and forties no longer needs to be part of our lives. Unless we chose it, of course, which we often do out of habit.

We can always keep busy. Our children and grandchildren are happy to allow us to continue to take care of them. There is always more stuff to buy so we have to work hard to pay for it. Every volunteer organization is looking to our generation as a source of workers.

I am not suggesting you quit doing any of those things. An active, joyful life is one of the things that keeps us vital. Just ask yourself why you are doing these things. Are they serving you? Are they fostering your soul? Do you have time left in your day for quiet contemplation and listening?

Many years ago when I was a science student, I was intrigued by the fact that they named various principles of science after the person who discovered them. What fun, I thought, to have a law named after you. So, being me, I made up my own set of laws. Thus I present to you Harwig's law number one: "It is far easier to get into things than out of them."

When I first started practicing law I joined a number of organizations and boards, mostly as a method of practice building. But, even after my practice was built

I continued to run around from meeting to meeting and group to group. Then one day I sat down and took a long hard look at my life. "What," I asked myself, "am I enjoying doing? What groups do I truly support and love? Which am I attending out of purely obligation or habit?"

A basic law of the universe (Harwig's law number two) is that "all things grow and change." As we grow and change, it becomes important to make sure that the things and people we are involved with are in the same place we are. As we age and take the time to examine our lives, we often find that we are simply in a different spot than we used to be and that the activities, friends, and hobbies we used to enjoy no longer fit us.

Then comes the hardest part … getting out. It took me years to resign from all my various boards and activities, but it was one of the very best things I have ever done. I gave myself the gift of time and the ability to choose what I did and with whom I did it.

As a member of the elder generation, you may find yourself in similar circumstances, where people and things no longer "fit." If that is so, it is okay to change what you do and who you see, even if other people in your life do not approve. (Harwig's law number three: "Nobody likes everything you do.")

So what, you may be asking, has this got to do with being psychic? The more I teach the intuitive path, the more certain I become that clarity is one of the most important traits to cultivate in our lives. We need to have clarity of thought in order to know what is truly intuitive and what is not. We need clarity of purpose to know what we really want out of our lives. Time is a gift given to us and we should not squander it on meaningless things. Remember, *we* are the ones who get to define what is meaningful to us.

Create a space in your life for quiet and solitude, and your intuition will meet you there.

CULTIVATE SILENCE

As we age, we need a lot more quiet. Our brains, as we become increasingly psychic, also need time and quiet to process the new information we are receiving. Quiet time, however, is difficult to find in this world. We need to seek out silence.

Just about every morning I take a three- or four-mile walk. When the weather is nice I always walk outside, enjoying the feel of the air on my skin, the scents that tickle my nose, and the myriad of sounds that play a quiet serenade in the background. It is one of my favorite times of the day and I have found that my best ideas, inspirations, intuitions, and conversations with my guides come during these strolls.

Walking like that always puts me in a light trance. I am still aware of my surroundings and yet I am somewhat detached from them. It is a perfect state in which to commune with my guides and to get psychic insights. I highly recommend it to anyone who is wondering what they can do to best enhance their intuition.

I meet a lot of people out on my walks and I am always surprised to see how many people walk while listening to iPods or other distractions. It surprises me because silent solitary walking provides a perfect opportunity to do something great for our bodies while also getting useful information from our psyches and souls. It is the ultimate in multitasking!

Yet, so many of us are seemly terrified of silence. An interesting experiment is to notice how often, if ever, you are in a silent environment. Most people are always surrounded by artificial noise whenever possible. Our radios, televisions, cell phones, and computers are always turned on, often at the same time. And then people ask me why they cannot hear their guides or spirits.

Guides and spirits are rather like background music in a noisy shopping center. If you listen carefully you can hear them, perhaps even pick out words or messages. But, most of the time, we are totally oblivious to both the guides and the music. Our intuitive minds hear them, of course, but we have no conscious knowledge or memory of the information we receive.

So, if you want to hear your intuition, you need to be quiet. Seems pretty simple, doesn't it?

It is also rather useful to have a time (whether walking or sitting) where you *intend* to listen to your intuition. Just let the conversation play in your mind and accept whatever you hear or whatever you think. It is good if this can be done on a regular basis. Guides and spirits have lives too, you know. Sometimes they are busy or off on an adventure. I often chuckle when I think of them saying, "Yeah, she never calls unless she is in trouble or wants something."

I love technology. I love music. But they are tools. Turn them off every once in a while and see what else there is to hear.

EMBRACE SIMPLICITY

We often use the word "simplicity" without really knowing what it means to us. The dictionary is of little help, simply stating it is a "condition or quality of being simple." It goes on, though, to state that simplicity can mean "freedom from hardship, effort, or confusion." I like that. When we use our intuition and trust what it tells us, our lives become simpler. As they say in twelve-step groups, "We intuitively know what used to baffle us."

I have made a decision to live my life with effortless ease. I cannot tell you I always follow that promise, but I can tell you that it remains a sort of benchmark for me. When I have a decision to make, I ask what I call my simplicity question. It is: "Will this thing (person, activity, purchase, etc.) aid or detract from my freedom and simplicity?" Whether it is a decision about going to an event, purchasing something, or meeting someone new, you *will* get an answer if you ask that question.

Sometimes decisions have to be broken down into several components and the question asked many times. For example, perhaps you are considering lending money to a family member. There are dozens of things to consider about this decision. It affects your relationship with the person, your financial state now and in the future, your self-esteem, and many other factors. While you are weighing those factors, though, add this one to it. Will this decision allow me to feel free and unburdened? You can break it down further. Will I feel more free and unburdened in how I interact with this person? Will I feel free and unburdened in how much money I have today? Will I feel free and unburdened in how secure I feel about the future? And so on. Your intuition will tell you the truth, if you are willing to listen.

Simplicity is different for each person. Some people feel most comfortable surrounded by many things and with a lot of people around them. Others of us, particularly as we age, have a strong desire to cleanse our lives of superfluous things that are cluttering up our spaces, our brains, and our hearts. No one can or should tell you what you should keep or get rid of. That choice is yours. Using the simplicity question, though, will allow your intuition to guide you.

MAKE A SPACE OF YOUR OWN

When I was a little girl, I shared a room with my older sister, Ruthie. It was, of course, *her* room, and I just got to sleep in it. When I was twelve, we moved to a larger house with three whole bedrooms. By then, though, I had a younger sister and once again had to share a room. I waited and counted the days until

Ruthie went away to college and I could actually get my own room.

I was fourteen when that day came. I remember it vividly. I suspect I was moving into Ruthie's room before her car had pulled out of the driveway. It was small and filled with overlarge unmatched furniture... but it was *mine*. For four blissful years (well, the years themselves were not blissful, but having my own room was), I had my own space. I could shut my door and keep the world out. I even had a secret hiding space that my little sister didn't know about. I dusted that room and cared for it like the treasure it was.

Then I went away to college and moved into a dorm where I shared a tiny room with my high school best friend and a bathroom with dozens of not-so-best friends. At the ripe old age of twenty-one, I married and moved into a one-bedroom apartment with my husband. After a few years we bought a tiny two-bedroom house. The extra bedroom became a television room.

And so it went. A few years later, we moved "up" to a four-bedroom house. With no children, a room of my own was certainly possible. By that time, though, I had forgotten the joy of having my own space. Things expanded into the unused space. The extra bedrooms became guest rooms and storage rooms while my husband and I lived primarily in two or three rooms of our seven-room house.

Like many of you, I had forgotten my need for private space. As I entered midlife, something seemed missing. I went on a rather classic midlife journey in search of Me. Along the way, I figured out that I needed a space of my own.

Some may think I overdo it nowadays. My husband and I own side-by-side townhouses. I not only have my own room, I have my own house. While I love him and love being with him, I also love having my own place. It works for us.

As we age, we need a place we can go and shut the door. We crave a private space where we can keep our stuff separate from our day-to-day lives. As much as we love our friends, spouses, and families, there is a time in our lives when we also desire to shut them out for a bit.

In our society, it is rare not to have a space you can call your own. It doesn't really matter how large a space you live in. Visit a homeless shelter sometime and watch how, even there, people often make a little *nest* for themselves. Having a space of our own is an intrinsic and natural craving that intensifies as we age.

Over a century ago, Virginia Woolf wrote the classic book *A Room of One's Own*. Her premise was that creative women needed a locked room in which to work. She stated "for the power to contemplate...a lock on the door means the power to think for oneself."

I agree with Virginia. Maybe you aren't able to have a room with a lock. But no matter how you live, you can create your own "nest." Find a place and declare it to be your contemplation space. You may need to use a space that is jointly used. If so, declare it to be yours for a few uninterrupted hours each day. For example, claim your bedroom as off limits between eight p.m. and nine p.m. Have a drawer at least, and a room preferably, that no one but you can enter without permission. Set your boundaries, and you will find that others will honor them.

FIND (OR CREATE) A COMMUNITY

Just when I tell you to become less busy, I also tell you to add something to your life. I admit the contradiction. The questionnaires all echo two themes though. Those of the elder generation crave two things: solitude and community.

The community we crave as we enter the elder generation is usually different from that which we have had in the past. As we age we often find we no longer desire to attend the same gatherings, meetings, or religious services that we used to love. Instead, we strongly desire to enter into a new type of community with people who accept our psychic gifts and encourage us to use them.

Vicki described this craving well. She said, "I can't really say there was a defining moment or trigger (when she felt her intuition increase). It has been a gradual feeling of being drawn to the idea of wanting to develop psychic abilities. I want the skills very much but don't know how to develop them. I am alone most of the time. I don't have friends that would share the same interest. I travel a lot for my job so I am unable to attend seminars and training. So, I just 'wish' and hope that someday when I retire I will be able to pursue it further."

As we claim our place in the elder generation, we are drawn to different interests, people, and activities. Many of the respondents to my questionnaire stressed that they had developed new friends and surrounded themselves with people who understood them. As Mary put it: "I now have new friends who are on a spiritual quest with me. It is great to talk and learn and discuss this together. They actually know and understand me better than my old friends of many years."

Often, our belief systems evolve. We may remain a part of a certain religious community or worship in the same way, but our beliefs tend to expand beyond the borders of a church. Mary wrote: "I've always been a Protestant Christian churchgoer. Now I listen differently. My image of Jesus has evolved. I think he was the ultimate psychic and very connected to a spirit world. If anything, I'm a stronger believer because I see the bigger picture better than when I was more skeptical."

One of the frustrations that many of us feel is that we do not know how to find a community of like-minded people. As Lucinda wrote to me, "In my fantasy world, there would be a gathering of queens and crones with our particular gestalt, to assess these gifts and plot our evolutionary course forward. Since we tend to crop up in social isolation (i.e., we're only a handful in a thousand), it's easier for us to think we are abnormal (since we are not the norm). It's difficult to find mentoring on the power of the gifts we have. That is unfinished work."

In fact, this is one of the motivators I had for writing this book. By giving a name to this phenomenon, I hope that it encourages some of you to start to form voluntary communities to discuss the changes that are happening to you. These communities can be as simple as a book discussion group or as complex as forming new ways of living together.

Four years ago a few of us started a meeting we call the Intuitive Forum. It was designed to be a once a month gathering where we would have a speaker who would discuss various alternative or metaphysical ideas, followed by a time where I would channel my guides and answer questions. In addition, it was meant to be a place where people could meet with and enjoy the company of others of like mind.

When we started the group we expected perhaps twenty or so attendees and were surprised and delighted when it rather quickly grew to attract over a hundred people. It is an example of the hunger in our land for a place to gather and discuss ideas that you may not feel comfortable talking about elsewhere.

If you can't find a community like this in your neighborhood, why not start one? Part of being a member of the elder generation is becoming a leader, a sage, a wise one. Perhaps you will find that your calling is to create this type of community.

CLAIM YOUR POWER

One of my favorite songs is KT Tunstall's "Suddenly I See." KT sings of a woman who "holds you captivated in her power." She goes on to describe this woman (whose face has aged to be a "map of the world") as having "the power to be, the power to give, the power to see." These beautiful lyrics perfectly describe for me what power is…and what I want it to look like in my own life.

One of the major steps that we must take as elders is to claim our power. Older people (in Western society, at least) tend to become invisible. While we control the vast majority of the wealth and make many of the purchasing decisions in our families, we are generally ignored by the media and the marketing community. With very few exceptions, models, actors, and even newscasters need to be young to be hired.

This book was not written to complain about that fact. It is our fault. We have the power. Why aren't we using it?

I believe that most of us are afraid of power. As we age, many of us have escaped from the corporate or governmental working world at least partially because of abuses of power. We watch the unfolding sagas of the political and business arenas in horror as we see power being misused. No wonder we avoid the topic.

But there are two types of power. There is power *over* and then there is power *to*. I think it is fair to say that many of us are uncomfortable with having power over another person or group. We are also perhaps wise enough to know that this type of power tends to corrupt a relationship. As much as we want to influence and help others, we realize that people have a right and responsibility to make their own decisions and live their own lives.

Power to is a very different thing. We all have the power *to* make a difference in our own lives and therefore in the lives of others. Having power to do things is an innate gift we are given and one we want to nurture. In a basic sense, we all have power. We have the power to move, speak, think, and act. Beyond that, however, we have the power to create our own lives. If we deny or run away from that power, it doesn't disappear. It just lies there, dormant and unused.

There are many things we are powerless over. Despite how hard we try, we are generally powerless over other people. Sometimes we get confused about the difference between the ability to influence others and having power over others. All of us influence other people by example and wisdom. As we members of the elder generation step into our own power, we can be a strong positive influence on other people and on the world.

Power over, in contrast, is usually abusive. Sometimes it is necessary. We lock criminals in prison to take away their power. We sometimes need to physically restrain children to keep them from hurting themselves. Still, most often power over is seen as abuse. It is therefore frightening to those of us who recognize that fact.

On a recent trip to Greece, I was once again taught a lesson about power. I was leading a spiritual journey with twenty-four travelers in my care. Our flight was delayed out of Minneapolis for three hours, giving us just minutes to make our connecting flight in Newark and on to Athens. The airline assured us that they would hold the flight to Athens for us, but, when we breathlessly arrived at the gate in Newark, we were informed that the airplane door had been shut and our seats filled with standby passengers. Furthermore, the next flight to Athens was a day and a half later.

With twenty-four travelers to be responsible for and fearing we would miss our Greek island cruise, I rushed to speak to someone with more authority than the gate agent. As I hunted down and spoke to a manager, I was surprised at how calm I felt. I was able to state quietly and yet powerfully that this situation was simply unacceptable. We must, I explained, board that plane and continue our journey.

For a moment it felt as if the air actually seemed to shift. At some level I knew that I could change this situation strictly with my words and my power. As I spoke confidently, clearly, and calmly, I could see the expression on the manager's face change from hostile to sympathetic. Yes, he agreed, it *was* unacceptable for us not to board the aircraft.

An hour later, we all had seats, our luggage was loaded and we were on our way to a magical and marvelous adventure in Greece. Despite all the delays, the flight arrived on time—and I had a lesson in the appropriate use of power.

This story reminds me of the scene in a *Star Wars* movie where Obi-Wan Kenobi used only his voice to gain entry into a city. Just as Obi-Wan demonstrated, it seemed that the very tone of my voice allowed no other option except the acceptable one. It was a situation where power was needed and could be used. It was the right thing to do and the only thing to do.

As these types of things happen to me, I become more and more comfortable with my use of power. I am realizing that power to do things is our birthright. It is not power over others. Rather, it is the power to claim what is rightfully ours. It is the power to *be* and to speak our truth. It is one of the gifts of being a part of the elder generation.

Exploring our power is fun. Learning where our power ends is valuable. As a generation of elders and wise ones, claiming our power is crucial.

twelve

....

Advice from the Elder Generation

Part of becoming sages, wise ones, and elders is passing on our wisdom to the next generation. In my questionnaire, I asked: What knowledge or skill would you most like to pass on to the next generation? The responses I received were wise and insightful. They tell, without any editing, of the wisdom that the elder generation has to share. Just as the elders in Native tribes are given the job of passing on wisdom, so do those of us who have awakened and can now listen to the voice of the universe.

Several themes emerged, though, from this collective wisdom. The first and perhaps foremost is: *We are one and we are guided.*

Here are some examples:

> "That we are all connected. That each of us is part of the All, and that we can care for ourselves and others in that way. Love each other. All of us."

> "That we are all one."

> "All paths lead to God."

> "Knowingness of the assistance we receive on this life's journey."

> "Taking time to listen to the still, small voices that are here to assist us."

> "Souls are eternal and we are all connected."

> "Joy and love, and the flexibility of the willow tree in the wind. We live in a river of connection."

> "Other than being human, we all look the same from our soul's perspective. We all come from the same source. The glow inside of us is our soul. The connection we share only varies by the strength of our connection to the universe around us."

> "You are not alone. We are all connected."

> "The knowledge that we are all energy. This energy is a collective energy. We are individuals yet we are all one. If we could all harness positive energy we could change the world."

The second theme is one dear to my heart. It is: *Be yourself.*

"Be true to yourself, and remember/know what's real. I believe it is important to be one's self. Many problems exist because people are not comfortable with who they are and do not want to get to know themselves. Our culture sends many mixed messages and people don't spend enough time learning about themselves for a variety of reasons."

"That everything we need to know, we already do."

"Awareness, sensitivity, imagination, listening to the soul, listening to the earth, and being authentically in tune with who we are as unique creations."

"Don't deny who you are, it makes life too difficult, embrace it."

"To trust their own instincts/intuition and not to live their life according to someone else's dogma."

"The knowledge that each of us is unique and wonderful and beautiful in our own way. That societal pressure to conform, and especially to *look* a certain way, are just that…society's pressures."

"Owning my intuition…completes me."

"Believe in yourself, and be charitable towards others. We must come to accept ourselves and recognize that we all have foibles and short-comings. We also have things we do well and they should be our focus. Accept yourself and don't put yourself down as you are a snowflake among others and unique and should be treasured."

"That it does not matter what anyone else thinks of you. If they judge you ... that is *their* issue."

"I would teach them how to block energy and not merge with people like I did."

"You have the right to say not now, especially when you want to, some just want to mess with you as a sibling, some as your enemy, some are sincere, if you feel icky it is icky and say be-gone."

"Treat your body well, for it is God/The Source's connection to the "thinker" within you. The more positive you are, by fighting that sneaky negative nature, the better you will feel and the more level you will be with your emotions."

"To always feel good about themselves despite what others may think of them."

Another theme that arose was love of and being in nature:

"Love of nature. I think our children have a nature deficit disorder."

"Be kind to the earth and its inhabitants."

"Let nature speak in a way we can hear, without mistrusting ourselves."

Of course, many of the respondents spoke of *intuitive knowing*:

"I would share that the ability to be intuitive is inside each one. Nurturing that ability, practicing it, and believing in yourself is the greatest gift that you can give to yourself. I wish someone had taught me that early in my life. Perhaps I would have been wiser earlier, and could have saved myself some heartbreak. But then, I wouldn't be who I am today without all the experiences I have lived with, so I guess everything is perfect…just like it is!"

"I would love to teach the world that we can believe in miracles and to look for signs all around us."

"The skill of listening to one's instinct/intuition above all else."

"To be open…to be tuned in to ones' self and use all of their senses. To follow their leads and most of all *trust*."

"Be comfortable with your gifts, have no fear of them, develop and use them."

"How to open your mind to incoming thoughts and feelings."

"I would pass on the gift of listening and awareness."

"The ability to know when you are in danger and to sense people who are not good for you."

"Enjoy your abilities and acknowledge them."

"The skill to *not* lose this ability (intuition) I believe we are born with and are taught to ignore."

"The skill to trust your gut instinct!"

"How to raise their vibrational level, develop, and deal with their psychic abilities, to help kids out who have psychic abilities but are frightened and misunderstood, as well as educating their parents and having a research component to look up the information these kids are getting to help validate for them and their parents that this is real and help them make connections with each other so they don't feel so alone. People need to stop being afraid of psychic abilities and need to be educated about it. I also want people to know how to use their energy and thoughts to make this a better world...universe and beyond. People need to know the power they have within them and how to use it to benefit. Everyone needs to raise their vibrational level!"

"To *believe* that there is so much more to life than we realize! We just need to learn to harness it. It would make the world a more peaceful place, no doubt."

"If nothing else—Listen and pay attention to those gut feelings or that little voice inside of you that lets you know when something just isn't right or better yet, lets you know that something is right. It makes life so much easier when you learn to trust those feelings and to trust yourself."

"The knowledge I would like to pass on to the next generation is to trust their psychic abilities, and to know that there are spirits around all of us to help us and teach us. They have a rich history of intuitive folks in their family."

"Listen to yourself, and if something does not feel right, stick with your intuition. Your soul is guiding you and knows what is best for you."

"An understanding of what is unseen, an acceptance of it, how to use it for positive action in their lives, and learning to tell the difference of good and bad related to same."

"The insight to know that the answers we all seek can be found within … and that we all have intuitive ability. We are here for two things … to love and to learn."

The theme of *creating our own lives* with our intentions and thoughts was also present in many of the responses:

"I would love to pass on to the next generation the skill of intention. How with love in our hearts we can work miracles every day. I would like them to know that they are putting negativity out in the universe with every negative thought. I believe in collective thoughts. We can change the world with good thoughts. We could heal, and learn powers we have never heard of. I believe the day will come when we can be anywhere in an instant, and talk through mental telepathy."

"The skill of deliberate creation of our life experience by at all times being consciously aware of our emotional state and purposefully choosing positive emotions, or at least emotions that feel better than those that we humans have a tendency to dredge up simply by observing our conditions. Focusing on better feelings and thoughts."

"The knowledge that we have personal power in shaping our lives and our health. How we train our minds to think about ourselves is very important. We can heal some of our own illness by changing our thought patterns. Also, we might not be able to see something but there is a spirit leading and guiding us."

"The knowledge that we are here together but only for a short time; that there is nothing to fear in death, it is only the doorway back home. I would like all people to know that creating in fear is not what we planned when we came to this life, but instead to re-know and begin to create only with love and joy in who we are and in what we can do together."

"Healing and the power of thoughts, to ideas, to action to being (manifestation)."

"Learn to connect with and listen to your heart. This is one of the most glorifying skills you can possess. Your heart will never lie to you. Not to say you can't be confused and feel it in your heart. I would hope that people can see their own faith in the messages we as intuitives offer. The time you take to make this connection as solid as possible ensures your intuition to be receiving information at the highest vibration and for your highest and best good."

Many people spoke of the wonder of being able to *communicate with the other side*:

"I think we can all be closer to the other side. The veil is thinning."

"That death is not a barrier to relationships."

"If you see a person or persons who are transparent or about to be transparent, they have already started to transition and are on their way out. The older generation changes their minds, but the young and transparent have already fulfilled their contracts and are transitioning."

"We do not die. Life goes on, although in another form. We are with our loved ones and they are with us forever."

"More of a knowing... Love never dies... We are always being guided."

"I think it is imperative that we (our generation) pass on the knowledge and information that we know about the world that we live in. The 'veil' is thinner than ever and our young 'feel' far more than we ever did."

I think that it is very important that all people come to know that those (human beings and animals) who have 'passed over' are really present to us if we are open. Our spirit/essence/soul is very much alive, as is the God who created us.

"To be open to the beings in the next dimension, and be open to feelings you have that may tell you that a spirit is nearby."

Being in the moment was a gift many wished to pass on to the next generation:

"The gift of presence, how important it is in communication and enjoying life. How valuable and powerful the present moment is, and how little our culture experiences it."

"If I could pass on only one gift to the next generation, it would be to enjoy the now ... and to know it is always now."

They also discussed living simply:

"On a practical level the information they need to survive, on a spiritual level to understand what is really important in life ... it isn't material things."

"Material things don't bring lasting joy. Joy comes from inside out."

"I would like future generations to learn that they are not what they have, or what education they have or how much money they have."

Others spoke of *how to treat others*:

"I would pass on the ability to help others."

"If you are able to feel someone's energy, you will likely know whether to trust or not, like or not. Many people are judged by how they look—we need to get past that and 'feel' the person."

"To be more in-tune and not so self-centered."

"Please, please, please, do not underestimate the power of kindness. Be more patient with others. Understand your responsibility and accountability for your actions and that everything you do matters on some level whether you know it or not. Know you are never, ever alone, even when you most feel alone. Know that whatever you are going through is temporary. Your worst struggles may someday be the very things you cherish most."

"*Never* judge a person until you have walked a mile in his shoes. We have become so judgmental in our society and we should stop that and accept each other and allow everyone to go their own way, as long as they do not hurt anyone else."

"Be charitable and help others. I feel that is one mark of a person that is important in loving yourself and others. It isn't how much you give, but that you try. You cannot cure the world's problems, but you can help."

"Time and love are what are important to children."

"My feelings I have about people. My son is a bit too trusting and I would love for him to be able to discern who is good and who is not."

"Cultivate friends and relationships always. I know that this is important because I haven't done it."

"It would be the ability to communicate in and with unconditional love and understanding both in our speaking and our listening. There are many layers to this superlative and supreme dynamic that enhances and optimizes every aspect of our person; from our senses to our sensitivities and ultimately how we communicate, commune and live in community with each other. It is what frees us to know, grow and discover all it means to be and become fully human and fully alive."

And, of course, many advised quiet time in *prayer and meditation*:

"Meditation is very important. Pray often."

"To learn how to get quiet and centered within yourself so you are better able to recognize the signals that come to us intuitively. Know that feelings are real indicators of energy and events happening around us. You just need to slow down and learn to recognize them. Trust yourself to act on your hunches."

"Spend time in quiet meditation and contemplation."

"That when we take the time to calm ourselves and withdraw to our internal selves for reflection, we pick up a lot of information from others and the universe, which I call God. And we can heal our systems by listening to what we hear when we slow ourselves down."

Finally, many urged the future generation to avoid fear.

"I would love to pass along the knowledge that fear is the real enemy—and that overcoming fear will open unimaginable doorways."

"Live in no fear. If so desired, choose a spiritual community to participate with that does not teach fear, or identification with ourselves as wretched, sinful, etc., but rather as magnificent, loving, wonder-full beings who, once we transcend ego (or at least consciously diminish ego), can experience true joy, purer service, and bliss."

"Acknowledging intuition provides a fear-free life."

"Belief that there are things that cannot be explained scientifically. That the path to joy and happiness is open and only blocked by our own fears."

As I read through this marvelous chapter of advice from the elder generation, I find myself wishing that this wisdom could be taught as a grade school or high school course. Imagine a world in which our youth are taught the truly important things in life at a young age.

It can happen. All it takes is for those of us with courage and conviction to step forward and tell our stories and claim our place as the wisdom keepers and elders that we are.

Blessings,
Kathryn

appendix

....

The Elder Generation Questionnaire

Your name (first only is fine)

_____

Date _____

Phone _____

E-mail _____

May Kathryn use your real name in the book?

_____

May Kathryn call you if she needs more information?

_____

How old are you? _____

Do you feel that you have psychic ability?

_____

At what age did you first feel this ability?
Please describe.

_____

_____

_____

_____

Do you feel that your interest in psychic things and/
or your psychic ability has changed since or around
age fifty?

_____

_____

_____

Did anything happen to prompt or trigger these abilities or change in abilities? If so, please describe.

_____

_____

Have you experienced any of the following after you were (approximately) fifty years old? (please check all that apply)

❑ Death of a child

❑ Loss of an important job or interest

❑ A sudden, life-changing event, such as divorce

❑ Serious emotional difficulty, such as depression

If so, did you sense an increase in intuitive or psychic abilities during or after any of these happenings? Please describe.

_____

_____

_____

_____

Have you noticed any of the following in yourself, particularly after age fifty? Please check all that apply.

❑ Desire to spend more time alone

❑ Desire to spend more time in prayer or meditation

❑ Change in sleep habits

❑ Less interest in day-to-day life and money concerns

❑ A change in friendships or interests in friendships

- ❏ A desire for a new spiritual community

- ❏ Reading the obituaries more often

- ❏ Your taste in books, magazines, and movies has changed

- ❏ More vivid dreams

- ❏ A knowing when things will happen

- ❏ A fear of certain people for no reason

- ❏ A liking of certain people without knowing them well

- ❏ Acting on your gut instincts more often

- ❏ A feeling of being isolated or different than others

- ❏ A sense of disapproval from family or friends

- ❏ A desire to learn more about mystical matters

- ❏ Anxiety or nervousness for no reason

- ❏ Seeing signs: birds, coins appearing, or other things that seem to have messages for you

- ❏ Electronic things sometimes work strangely around you

- ❏ Having things disappear and reappear for no reason

- ❏ Knowing who is calling before picking up the phone

- ❏ Feelings of forgetfulness about unimportant things

Have you noticed any changes in yourself since you turned fifty that have not been mentioned above? Please expand.

_____

_____

_____

_____

Have you noticed any changes in the way your friends and/or family treat you since these changes and awakened abilities? Please discuss.

_____

_____

_____

_____

Have you ever felt direct contact or conversation with a spirit (deceased person)? If so, please discuss.

_____

_____

_____

_____

_____

Have you taken any steps to enhance, learn, or control your psychic ability? If so, discuss.

_____

_____

_____

_____

What knowledge or skill would you most like to pass on to the next generation?

_____

_____

_____

_____

TO WRITE TO THE AUTHOR

If you wish to contact the author or would like more information about this book, please write to the author in care of Llewellyn Worldwide Ltd., and we will forward your request. Both the author and publisher appreciate hearing from you and learning of your enjoyment of this book and how it has helped you. Llewellyn Worldwide Ltd. cannot guarantee that every letter written to the author can be answered, but all will be forwarded. Please write to:

Kathryn Harwig
℅ Llewellyn Worldwide Ltd.
2143 Wooddale Drive
Woodbury, MN 55125-2989

Please enclose a self-addressed stamped envelope for reply, or $1.00 to cover costs. If outside the U.S.A., enclose an international postal reply coupon.

GET MORE AT LLEWELLYN.COM

Visit us online to browse hundreds of our books and decks, plus sign up to receive our e-newsletters and exclusive online offers.

- **Free tarot readings • Spell-a-Day • Moon phases**
- **Recipes, spells, and tips • Blogs • Encyclopedia**
- **Author interviews, articles, and upcoming events**

GET SOCIAL WITH LLEWELLYN

Follow us on

www.Facebook.com/LlewellynBooks

www.Twitter.com/Llewellynbooks

GET BOOKS AT LLEWELLYN

LLEWELLYN ORDERING INFORMATION

Order online: Visit our website at www.llewellyn.com to select your books and place an order on our secure server.

Order by phone:
- Call toll free within the U.S. at 1-877-NEW-WRLD (1-877-639-9753)
- Call toll free within Canada at 1-866-NEW-WRLD (1-866-639-9753)
- We accept VISA, MasterCard, and American Express

Order by mail:
Send the full price of your order (MN residents add 6.875% sales tax) in U.S. funds, plus postage and handling to: Llewellyn Worldwide, 2143 Wooddale Drive Woodbury, MN 55125-2989

POSTAGE AND HANDLING:

STANDARD: (U.S., Mexico & Canada)
(Please allow 2 business days)
$25.00 and under, add $4.00.
$25.01 and over, FREE SHIPPING.

INTERNATIONAL ORDERS (airmail only):
$16.00 for one book, plus $3.00 for each additional book.

Visit us online for more shipping options. Prices subject to change.

FREE CATALOG!

To order, call
1-877-NEW-WRLD
ext. 8236
or visit our website